The
PERFORMANCE
Manager

Proven Strategies for Turning Information into Higher Business Performance

by Roland Mosimann, Patrick Mosimann, and Meg Dussault

The PERFORMANCE Manager

Proven Strategies for Turning Information into Higher Business Performance

Edited by
John Blackmore

Production and Launch Team:
Carrie Bendzsa
Steve Hebbs
Lars Milde
Randi Stocker

Printed in Canada, 2007. ISBN 978-0-9730124-1-5

INTRODUCTION

The Performance Manager continues an exploration that began more than ten years ago with the publication of *The Multidimensional Manager*. Both books examine the partnership between decision-makers in companies worldwide and the people who provide them with better information to drive better decisions.

More than a decade ago, the focus was on understanding an exciting new transformational trend—companies were becoming more *customer-* and *profit-centric*. What drove that trend? Companies were relying more and more on information assets such as business intelligence.

Today, that focus has become even sharper and more important. Global competition and interconnected global supply chains have further intensified downward pressures on cost. Technology and the Internet have transformed the knowledge economy from the equivalent of a specialty store into a 24/7/365 big-box retailer. Vast amounts of content are accessible anytime, anywhere.

Today, companies are expected to have a depth of insight into their customers' needs unheard of ten years ago. And yet market uncertainty is greater than ever. The pace of rapid change does not allow for many second chances. In other words, if being customer- and profit-centric was important then, it is critical now.

To better support the decision-maker/technology professional partnership, *The Multidimensional Manager* introduced *24 Ways*, a set of business intelligence solutions used by innovative companies to drive greater profitability. These solutions were organized by business function and reflected the insight that the most valuable information in corporate decision-making is concentrated in a relatively small number of information "sweet spots", nodes in a corporation's information flow.

The book also introduced two further insights. First, the emergence of a new breed of manager—*the multidimensional manager*, who could effectively navigate and process these information sweet spots and thus make better, faster decisions. Second, the maturity of the enabling technology—business intelligence.

The book launched a fascinating dialogue. Demand led to the printing of more than 400,000 copies. People used it to help understand and communicate the promise of business intelligence. The pages often dog-eared and annotated, it became a field manual for business and IT teams tasked with developing solutions for their companies. Cognos (which commissioned the book), BI International (which co-authored it and developed the *24 Ways*), and the company PMSI (which partnered closely with both), maintained a dialogue with hundreds of companies over the years, collecting and synthesizing the many common experiences and refining them into a body of best practices and solution maps.

Ten years on, *The Performance Manager* revisits this dialogue and the underlying assumptions and observations made in the first book. We share our conclusions about what has changed and what has been learned by successful companies and managers in their attempts to drive profitability with better information. While the core principles originally presented have evolved, they are still largely true. After all, businesses exist to serve *customers*, and notwithstanding the tech boom's focus on market share, *profit* is the ultimate measure of success. *The Performance Manager* is not a sequel; though related, it stands on its own. We hope it will launch a new dialogue among those ambitious and forward-looking managers who view information not as a crutch but as a way to both drill down into detail and search outward into opportunity.

The Changing Value of Information

McKinsey Quarterly research since 1997[1] has followed an interesting trend that relates directly to the dialogue we started a decade ago. Based on this research, McKinsey distinguishes between three primary forms of work and business activity:

1. **Transformational work** – Extracting raw materials and/or converting them into finished goods

2. **Transactional work** – Interactions that unfold in a rule-based manner and can be scripted or automated

3. **Tacit work** – More complex interactions requiring a higher level of judgment involving ambiguity and drawing on tacit or experiential knowledge

In relation to the U.S. labor market, McKinsey drew several conclusions. First, tacit work has increased the most since 1998. It now accounts for 70 percent of all new jobs, and represents more than 40 percent of total employment. The percentage in service industries is even higher—for example, it's nearly 60 percent in the securities industry.

Second, over the same period investment in technology has not kept pace with this shift in work. Technology spending on transactional work was more than six times greater than spending on tacit work. This reflects the past decade's efforts in re-engineering, process automation, and outsourcing. It makes sense: linear, rule-based transactional processing is the easiest to improve.

---

[1] Bradford C. Johnson, James M. Manyika and Lareina A. Yee: "The next revolution in interactions," *McKinsey Quarterly* (2005, Number 4), and "Competitive advantage from better interactions," *McKinsey Quarterly* (2006, Number 2).

But McKinsey's third finding is the most important: competitive advantage is harder to sustain when it is based on gains in productivity and cost efficiency in transaction work. McKinsey's research found that industries with high proportions of tacit work also have 50 percent greater variability in company performance than those industries in which work is more transaction-based. In other words, the gap between the leaders and laggards was greatest in industries where tacit work was a larger proportion of total work.

This fascinating research confirms what most of us have known intuitively for some time. Our jobs have become more and more information-intensive—less linear and more interactive, less rule-based and more collaborative—and at the same time we are expected to do more in less time. While technology has helped in part, it hasn't achieved its full potential.

The Performance Manager can help this happen. It offers insights and lessons learned on leveraging your information assets better in support of your most valuable human capital assets: the growing number of high-value decision-makers. Given the right information-enabling technology and leadership, these decision-makers can become performance managers. Such managers deliver sustainable competitive advantage by growing revenue faster, reducing operational expenses further, and leveraging long-term assets better. The companies whose experiences we share in this book have validated this promise with hard-earned victories in the trenches.

Enabling Decision Areas that Drive Performance

This book synthesizes countless, varied company experiences to construct a framework and approach that others can use. The information sweet spot was the cornerstone concept of *The Multidimensional Manager*. Sweet spots, business intelligence, and multidimensional managers were the keys to the book's profitability promise.

These three insights are still fundamental to the promise of *The Performance Manager* and the need to leverage information assets to make high-value decisions that:

- Enable faster revenue growth
- Further reduce operational expenses
- Maximize long-term asset returns
- → and therefore deliver sustainable competitive advantage.

If anything, these three insights are even more critical to success today.

Insight 1 revisited: *The information sweet spot* → *More "sweet" required today*

In 1996, we wrote that "the most valuable information for corporate decision-making is concentrated in a relatively small number of *sweet spots* of information that flow through a corporation." The driving logic was the relative cost of acquisition and delivery of information versus the value and importance of that information. While this cost/benefit consideration is still valid, four factors require today's decision-making information to be defined, refined, and repackaged in even more detail than ten years ago:

1. *More:* There is simply much more information available today. The term "data warehouse" is no accident. Companies collect massive amounts of transaction data from their financial, supply chain management, human resources, and customer relationship management systems. Early on, often the problem was finding the data to feed business intelligence reports and analytics. Today, data overload is the greater challenge.

2. *Faster:* Information flow has become faster and more pervasive. The Internet, wireless voice and data, global markets, and regulatory reporting requirements have all contributed to a 24/7/365 working environment. Today's company is always open for business. Managers are always connected. Time for analysis, action, and reaction is short, especially in the face of customer demands and competitive pressures.

3. *Integrated:* Work has become more interactive and collaborative, requiring more sharing of information. This means integrating information across both strategic and operational perspectives as well as across different functional and even external sources.

4. *Enrichment:* Effective decision-making information requires more business context, rules, and judgments to enrich and refine the raw transaction data. Categorizations and associations of this data create valuable insights for decision-makers.

Insight 2 revisited: *Managers think multidimensionally* → *Managers perform within iterative and collaborative decision-making cycles*

Ten years ago, many multidimensional managers tended to be "power users" who were both willing and able to navigate through a variety of information to find the answers they needed. These users were adept at slicing and dicing *when*, *who*, *what*, and *where* to better understand results.

The ease of ad hoc discovery was incredibly powerful to managers previously starved for information and, more important, answers. This power of discovery is still highly relevant today, but the need for decision-making information has evolved: analysis by *some* isn't enough—what is required is interaction and collaboration by *all*. As the research by McKinsey shows, more and more tacit work is required to drive innovation and competitiveness. Today's performance managers include more executives, professionals, administrators, and external users, and are no longer mainly analysts.

Iterative and collaborative decision-making cycles result from more two-way interaction in common decision steps: setting goals and targets; measuring results and monitoring outcomes; analyzing reasons and causes; and re-adjusting future goals and targets. These two-way interactions can be framed in terms of different *decision roles* with different *work responsibilities* and *accountabilities* for a given set of decisions. These job attributes situate performance managers in a decision-making cycle that cuts across departmental silos and processes. This cycle clarifies their involvement in the information workflow, helping define the information they exchange with others in driving common performance goals. A decision role can be derived from a person's work function (such as Marketing, Sales, Purchasing, etc.) and/or their job type (such as executive, manager, professional, analyst, etc.).

Work responsibilities can be divided into three basic levels of involvement:

1. *Primary:* Decisions at this level are required to perform particular transactions or activities and are made often. Typically, this employee is directly involved, often in the transaction itself, and his/her activity directly affects output and/or cost, including for planning and control purposes. He/she has access to information because it is part of the job requirement.

2. *Contributory:* Information supports decisions made with indirect responsibility. Decisions are more ad hoc and may add value to a transaction or activity. The employee at this level may have to resolve a problem or, for example, adjust a production schedule based on sales forecasts.

3. *Status:* Information supports executive or advisory decisions. These people receive status updates on what is going on. Sometimes they manage by exception and get updates only when events fall outside acceptable ranges.

These different levels mean that securing sweeter information sweet spots is not enough. Information must be tailored to a person's decision role, work responsibility, and accountability for a given set of decisions. In the past, many business intelligence efforts stumbled precisely because of a one-size-fits-all approach to user adoption. Information must be packaged according to use and user role.

Insight 3 revisited: *The reporting paradigm for managers has changed → Performance managers need integrated decision-making functionality in varied user modes*

Business intelligence was an emerging technology in the mid 1990s. Today's business intelligence has matured to fit the notion of performance management. To fully support sweeter information sweet spots and collaboration within decision-making cycles, you need a range of integrated functionality. For performance managers with varied roles and responsibilities and those making decisions based on back-and-forth collaboration, functionality can't be narrowed to just one kind, such as scorecards for executives, business intelligence for business analysts, or forecasting for financial analysts. In practice, performance managers need a range of functionality to match the range of collaboration and interaction their job requires.

Every decision-making cycle depends on finding the answers to three core questions: *How are we doing? Why? What should we be doing?* Scorecards and dashboards monitor the business with metrics to find answers to *How are we doing?* Reporting and analysis provides the ability to look at historic data and understand trends, to look at anomalies and understand *Why?* Planning and forecasting help you establish a reliable view of the future and answer *What should we be doing?* Integrating these capabilities allows you to respond to changes happening in your business.

HOW ARE WE DOING?

Measuring and Monitoring

WHAT SHOULD WE BE DOING?

Planning

WHY?

Reporting and Analysis

To ensure consistency in answering these fundamental performance questions, you must integrate functionality not just within each one, but across them all. Knowing what happened without finding out why is of little use. Knowing why something happened but being unable to plan and make the necessary changes is also of limited value. Furthermore, this integrated functionality must be seamless across the full network of performance managers, whether within a department or across several. In this sense, the new paradigm today is the platform. Just as the questions are connected, the answers must be based on a common understanding of metrics, data dimensions, and data definitions, as well as a shared view of the organization. Drawing answers from disconnected sources obscures the organization's performance and hampers decision-making. Real value means providing a seamless way for decision-makers to move among these fundamental questions. The integrated technology platform is vital to connect people throughout the system to shared information. Its core attributes include the ability to:

• Integrate data from a variety of data sources

• Supply consistent information across the enterprise by deploying a single query engine

• Restrict information to the right people

• Package and define the information in business terms

You must also be able to present the information in a variety of user modes. Today many decisions are made outside the traditional office environment. The system must support the shifting behaviors of the business consumer. Decision-makers must be able to:

• Use the Internet to access information

• Use text searches to find key information sweet spots

• Create the information they need by using self-service options

• Set up automatic delivery of previously defined snippets of information

• Have guided access to the information they need so they can manage by exception

The *24 Ways* Revisited: *Decision Areas that Drive Performance*

Perhaps the single most powerful idea in *The Multidimensional Manager* was the *24 Ways*. Organized by functional department, these proven information sweet spots became a simple road map for countless companies to deploy business intelligence. This system was easy to communicate, notably to a business audience, and showed how operational results ultimately flowed back to the financial statements. Through hundreds of workshops and projects that followed the release of *The Multidimensional Manager*, BI International and PMSI became informal clearinghouses for ideas and feedback on the *24 Ways*. This was most notable in the BI University program, developed and launched by BI International and then acquired and operated by Cognos.

Starting in 2000, BI International and PMSI synthesized these experiences into a new, more refined and flexible framework to address the revisions to each of the insights noted above. Known as the DecisionSpeed® framework, it enables faster business intelligence *designs*, *deployments*, and ultimately *decisions*.

Expanded to include roughly twice as many sweeter information sweet spots as the 24 Ways, these decision areas are common to most companies. The framework is highly flexible, and circumstances will dictate how to best design and develop specific information sweet spots. You may require more detailed variations, in particular, other decision areas to meet specific needs. But the logic of each decision area is the same: to provide a simple, easy-to-understand way to drive performance—and also to measure, monitor, and analyze it, report on it, and plan for it.

The specific industry is also a key factor in the number and definition of decision areas. For this book, we chose and adapted a generic manufacturing industry model because it is the most common and broadly recognized.[4] While other industries may present a different set of specific decision areas, the business fundamentals in this book apply across most companies.

Decision areas are organized by the eight major functions of a company that drive different slices of performance. Though this is similar to the *24 Ways* functional map, there are some significant differences. An enlarged Operations function now combines the purchasing, production and distribution areas, reflecting the decade-long effect of integrated supply chains and business process improvement. Human Resources and IT now each have their own focus, as does Product Development.

These eight functions provide the core structure of the book. Starting with Finance, each chapter introduces some key challenges and opportunities that most companies face today. A recurring theme is that of striking the right balance among competing priorities. How to weigh different options, how to rapidly make adjustments—these are often more difficult decisions than coming up with the options in the first place. The decision areas for a particular function represent the information sweet spots best suited to it, for the balancing act required to meet challenges and exploit opportunities. In this book we have focused on some 46 decision areas, ranging from three to seven per function.

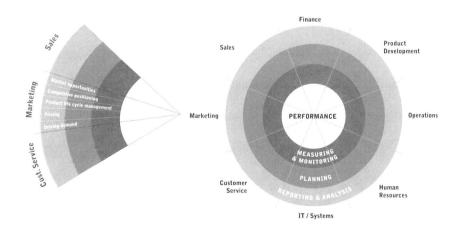

[4] Other industry models of the framework will be available in various follow-on programs and initiatives.

We introduce each decision area briefly, giving an illustration of the core content of the corresponding information sweet spot. These are organized into two types of measures: goals and metrics, and a hierarchical set of dimensions. While performance can be measured both ways, metrics typically offer additional detail for understanding *what* drives goal performance, especially when further described by dimensional context. A map of *which* performance managers are likely to use this decision area is included, showing relevant *decision roles* and *work responsibilities*.

The DecisionSpeed® framework is more than a list of sweeter information sweet spots. As the bull's-eye graphic implies, decision areas and functions are slices of a broader, integrated framework for performance management across the company. You can build the framework from the bottom up, with each decision area and function standing on its own.

INCOME STATEMENT DECISION AREA

GOALS	METRICS	DIMENSIONS
Actual vs. Plan Variance ($/%)	Fixed Costs ($/%)	Fiscal Month
Net Sales ($)	Gross Profit ($/%)	Year
Operating Profit/EBIT ($/%)	Interest ($/%)	Quarter
	Marketing Costs ($/%)	Month
	Material Costs ($)	Organization
	Material Margin ($/%)	Division
	Net Profit ($/%)	Department
	SG&A ($/%)	Org. Code
	Tax ($/%)	Plan/Actual Scenario
	Variable Costs ($/%)	Scenario
		Product Line
		Product Line

FUNCTION	DECISION ROLES	PRIMARY WORK	CONTRIBUTORY	STATUS
Finance				
	Executives	•		
	Managers	•		
	Analysts	•		
	Professionals	•		
Audit				
	Executives			•
	Managers	•		
	Professionals	•		
Customer Service				
	Executives		•	
Distribution				
	Executives		•	
Human Resources				
	Executives		•	
IT / Systems				
	Executives		•	
Marketing				
	Executives		•	

Over the past ten years, we have learned that you need a practical, step-by-step approach to performance management. Overly grand, top-down enterprise designs tend to fail, or don't live up to their full promise, due to the major technical and cultural challenges involved. This framework is designed for just such an incremental approach. You can select the one or two functional chapters that apply, much like a reference guide. Decision areas empower individual performance managers to achieve immediate goals in their areas of responsibility. As you combine these goals across decision areas, you create a scorecard for that function. Then, as you realize performance success, you can build upon it to solve the greater challenge posed by cross-functional collaboration around shared strategies and goals.

A key factor that makes this step-by-step approach work within a broader company perspective is the direct tieback to the financials included in the design. While each decision area can provide integrated decision-making functionality around its own set of issues, it also provides answers that impact financial results. Goals and metrics in non-financial decision areas, such as Sales, Marketing, or Operations, provide answers to financial statement numbers in the income statement, balance sheet, and cash flow, and help set future plans for growing revenue faster, reducing operational expenses further, and leveraging long-term assets better.

At the end of each chapter, we illustrate how each function can monitor its performance and contribute plans for future financial targets. Key goals and metrics for the function are shown for two decision areas outlined in the chapter. The planning process links them with the relevant dimensions, ensuring that resources are allocated and expectations set against financial and operational goals. For instance, "Company Share (%)" is planned out using the dimensions of time, region, market segment, and brand. This process changes the objective from an aggregate percentage share increase to a specific percentage share increase for a particular quarter, region, market segment, and brand. In this way, the planning process ties back from decision-making processes through the organization to the financials.

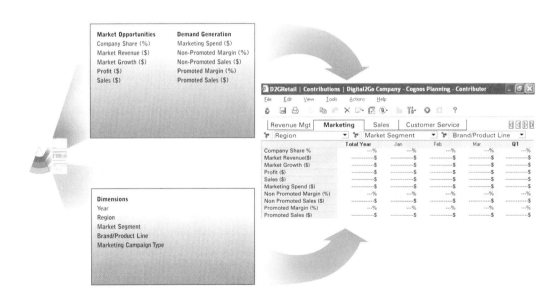

The Executive Management chapter outlines how different decision areas across multiple functions combine to drive shared strategic goals in the areas of financial management, revenue management, expense management, and long-term asset management. It also provides the top-down narrative for the overall framework.

A further objective of the DecisionSpeed® framework is to help define the decision-making process, or tacit work, described in the introduction. You can think of decision areas as a layer of information sweet spots that sit above the transaction flow in a related but non-linear fashion. As described in the Executive Management chapter, performance decisions often must combine input from across multiple processes, and do so in an iterative and non-linear fashion, in contrast to core transaction processes.

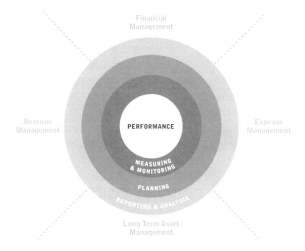

Here the framework is anchored in three back-to-basics concepts:

1. How does this tie back to the financials? (the *so what* question)

2. How does this tie back to organizational functions and roles? (the *who is accountable* question)

3. How does this fit with business processes? (the *where, when,* and *how* question)

Our jobs have become less linear and more interactive, requiring iteration and collaborative decision making. This requires the kind of information that drives high-performance decisions. This information is aggregated, integrated, and enriched across processes in a consistent way. It is grouped and categorized into information sweet spots designed to drive performance decisions. This is the information framework outlined in this book.

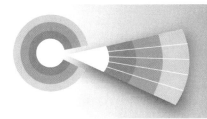

Trusted Advisor or Compliance Enforcer?

Can anybody remember when the times were not hard and money not scarce?
Ralph Waldo Emerson

Of all the various roles Finance can play in a company, the two most necessary to balance are complying with legal, tax, and accounting regulatory requirements and dispensing sound advice on the efficient allocation of resources. In the first, Finance must focus on checks and controls. In the second, it leverages its extensive expertise in understanding what resources are required to generate which revenues. It is uniquely positioned to play this second role because, while most business departments push as far as they can in a single direction, Finance must evaluate the company's contrasting realities.

How Finance strikes this balance (and many others) to a large measure determines the success or failure of the company. *Is your budget a tool to control costs, or to sponsor investment?* Depending on your industry, and where your company is in the market life cycle, one choice is better than the other.

Finance is the mind of the business, using a structured approach to evaluate the soundness of the many business propositions and opportunities you face every day. Information feeds this process, and Finance has more information than most departments. As it fills its role of balancing—aligning processes and controls while advising the business on future directions—Finance faces a number of barriers when it comes to information and how to use it.

Barrier 1: *Lack of information needed to regulate what has happened and shape what will happen*

Finance requires new levels of information about past and present processes and events to meet its regulatory compliance responsibilities. *Did the right employee or department sign off a particular expense item? Did customer credit checks take place before accepting and shipping an order?* For some companies, the information demands of compliance and control have forged better relationships between Finance and IT. They have led to changes in information gathering and collaboration methods (such as linking disconnected spreadsheets, for example), lowering the control risks these represent.

But while Finance works to manage these issues, it must also ensure the information investment helps drive its other key responsibility: helping guide decisions that make a difference to the future bottom line.

The executive team and sales reps both look to Finance to help the business plan its future with confidence, not simply manage money in and money out. Finance must pay attention to the drivers that make profit, using value-added analysis to extrapolate the impact of these drivers on tomorrow's results—and anticipate them when necessary.

Valuing, monitoring, and making decisions about intangible assets exemplifies the interconnection and sophistication of the information Finance requires. Regarding human capital, for example, Human Resources and Finance must work together to identify the value-creating roles of individuals, reflect their worth, and manage their growth, rewards, and expenses.

Without information sweet spots that show both the status of control and compliance and the impact of drivers on future business opportunities, Finance can't strike the necessary balance.

Barrier 2: *The relevance, visibility, and credibility of what you measure and analyze is designed for accounting rather than business management*

Finance collects, monitors, and reports information with distinct legal, tax, and organizational requirements to fulfill its fiduciary role. But Finance also needs an integrated view of these and other information silos to fill its role of advisor. This role requires not simply reporting the numbers but adding value to those numbers.

For example, international companies that operate across several countries usually separate sales and production entities. Without see-through profit, a local sales office may cut products that appear to be loss-making but in fact still make a marginal contribution to the production company's profit.

Another example: Marketing must understand spending on various activities. Finance must categorize relevant expense accounts across a wide range of detailed and hierarchically complex general ledger accounts. Without this comprehensive view, the same expense may be classified in different accounts by different individuals.

Barrier 3: *Finance must balance short term and long term, detailed focus and the big picture*

Finance balances different and contradictory requirements. It must deliver on shareholder expectations every 90 days; it must also determine a winning vision and a strategy to achieve that vision over quarters and years. Companies can cut costs and investments to meet short-term profit objectives, but at what point does this affect long-term financial health? A well-informed executive team is able to understand the drivers, opportunities, and threats when balancing short- and long-term financial performance.

Executives and financial analysts define performance in terms of shareholder value creation. This makes metrics such as earnings per share (EPS) growth or economic value added (EVA) important. However, these distilled financial measures tell only one piece of the story. You need to augment them with more detailed measures that capture sales, market share gains, and revenue growth targets to understand the real health of the company, and strike a good balance between long- and short-term growth.

Barrier 4: *Finance must find the path between top-down vision and bottom-up circumstances*

To what extent should goals be set top-down versus bottom-up? *If the executive team mandates double-digit profit growth, does this translate into sensible targets at the lower levels of the organization? Does it require a double-digit target at the lowest profit center?* Top-down financial goals must be adjusted to bottom-up realities. Finance must accommodate top-management vision while crafting targets that specific business units can achieve.

This barrier in particular illustrates the importance of engaging frontline managers in financial reporting, planning, and budgeting. The need for fast and relevant information requires an interactive model. Frontline managers must assume some budgetary responsibility and feed back changes from various profit or cost centers as market conditions change. This decentralized model engages the business as a whole rather than relying on a centralized function to generate information.

Besides freeing up Finance for value-added decision support, bottom-up participation generates an expense and revenue plan that overcomes hurdles of relevance, visibility, and credibility. Individuals who engage in the process take responsibility for delivering on expectations. This helps expose drivers of success and failure that are otherwise lost in a larger cost calculation or financial "bucket"—for both the frontline manager and Finance.

Balancing Short Term and Long Term, Past and Future, Compliance and Advisor

The information Finance uses to report what has happened and shape what will happen is critical to the rest of the organization. Dynamic tools that allow Finance to balance compliance and performance, accounting and business structures, short term and long term, top-down vision and bottom-up reality are more important than ever. Information sweet spots can support Finance's responsibilities and decision areas.

A Balanced Financial Experience

Finance decision areas:

- **Income statement →** How did the business team score; where was performance strong or weak?

- **Drill-down variance →** What causes changes in financial performance?

- **Operational plan variance →** How do we best support, coordinate, and manage the delivery of meaningful plans?

- **Cash flow and working capital →** How do we manage working capital, collect accounts receivables, and monitor cash use effectively?

- **Balance sheet →** How do we balance and structure the financial funding options, resources, and risks of the business?

- **CapEx and strategic investments →** What are the investment priorities and why?

- **Treasury →** How can we efficiently manage cash and liquidity requirements?

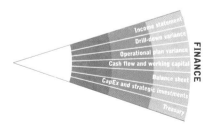

Income Statement

This decision area represents the bottom line. It is the cumulative score achieved by everyone in the business for a set period. Everyone needs to understand his or her individual contribution and performance measured against expectations.

You must understand where variances above budget occur so you can correct the course. If costs are increasing too quickly, you risk damaging future profits unless you control them, adjust selling prices, or develop new markets. Unexpected revenue spikes can mean additional resources are required to continue future growth. Adjustments such as these take time: the sooner you take action, the sooner you improve margins and realize the full potential of a growth opportunity. The ability of Finance to quickly identify, analyze, and communicate important variances has competitive implications for your company. How quickly the business capitalizes on a new situation is determined by how quickly it discovers budget variances.

GOALS	METRICS	DIMENSIONS
Actual vs. Plan Variance ($/%)	Fixed Costs ($/%)	Fiscal Month
Net Sales ($)	Gross Profit ($/%)	Year
Operating Profit/EBIT ($/%)	Interest ($/%)	Quarter
	Marketing Costs ($/%)	Month
	Material Costs ($)	Organization
	Material Margin ($/%)	Division
	Net Profit ($/%)	Department
	SG&A ($/%)	Org. Code
	Tax ($/%)	Plan/Actual Scenario
	Variable Costs ($/%)	Scenario
		Product Line
		Product Line

FUNCTION	DECISION ROLES	PRIMARY WORK	CONTRIBUTORY	STATUS
Finance				
	Executives	•		
	Managers	•		
	Analysts	•		
	Professionals	•		
Audit				
	Executives			•
	Managers		•	
	Professionals		•	
Customer Service				
	Executives		•	
Distribution				
	Executives		•	
Human Resources				
	Executives		•	
IT / Systems				
	Executives		•	
Marketing				
	Executives		•	
Operations / Production				
	Executives		•	
Purchasing				
	Executives		•	
Product Development				
	Executives		•	
Sales				
	Executives		•	

Each month, about 1.2 million records of financial information—income statements, invoice lines, and balance sheet analyses—from 80 sites are loaded into the system. Users feel encouraged to perform analyses without bothering about the nature of the original data source.

Nicolas Mathei, International IS Project Manager, Vesuvius Group

Drill-Down Variance

Once you identify a difference between actual and plan, you need to drill down into the details to understand what caused it. *If sales increase by five percent between two time periods, was the cause greater volume, higher price, or a change in the product mix? Did your competitors have the same increase in sales? If profits increased, was it due to increases in the cost of goods, a change in product mix to lower margin products, or a reduction in discretionary spending? Did your competitors experience the same increase?*

Finance needs to understand the *why* behind changes. Knowing what drove changes in revenue and profit provides a more complete picture to help guide the company.

GOALS	METRICS	DIMENSIONS
Profit Change ($/%)	Avg. Unit Cost ($) – Actual	Billing Customer
Sales Change ($/%)	Avg. Unit Cost ($) – St'd	Industry Group
Volume/Price/Mix Variance ($/%)	Discount (%)	Industry
	GL Expense Detail ($/%)	Category
	Net Change ($/%)	Customer Name
	Net Price ($)	Fiscal Month
	Net Sales ($)	Year
	Units Sold (#)	Quarter
		Month
		GL Lines
		Organization
		Division
		Department
		Org. Code
		Product SKU
		Product Line
		Brand
		SKU

FUNCTION	DECISION ROLES	PRIMARY WORK	CONTRIBUTORY	STATUS
Finance				
	Executives	•		
	Managers	•		
	Analysts	•		
	Professionals	•		
Audit				
	Executives			•
	Managers	•		
	Professionals	•		
Customer Service				
	Executives			•
	Analysts		•	
Distribution				
	Executives			•
	Analysts		•	
Marketing				
	Executives			•
	Analysts		•	
Operations / Production				
	Executives			•
	Analysts		•	
Purchasing				
	Executives			•
	Analysts		•	
Product Development				
	Executives			•

Operational Plan Variance

Once Finance understands what caused performance variances, it can lead discussions about future operating plans. The ability to advise and push back on management plans is important. Knowing the *why* behind variances from plan helps companies re-evaluate and improve the next plan.

Without this information, plans lose their purpose and become academic exercises to please senior management. Ideally, Finance offers input and feedback that other business areas can use for guidance. At the same time, these other areas provide frontline information to Finance that helps improve the plan. Such cross-functional and coordinated effort lets you test the roadworthiness of existing business plans.

GOALS	METRICS	DIMENSIONS
Operating Cost Variance ($/%)	Actual vs. Plan (%)	Fiscal Month
Overhead Cost Variance ($/%)	Avg. Unit Cost ($) – Actual	Year
Prod. Cost/Sales Ratio (%)	Avg. Unit Cost ($) – St'd	Quarter
	Distribution Cost ($/%)	Month
	Employees (#)	GL Lines
	Forecast ($)	Organization
	Labor Costs ($/%)	Division
	Marketing Costs ($/%)	Department
	Overhead Costs ($)	Org. Code
	Plan ($)	Plan/Actual Scenario
	Production Costs ($)	Scenario
	Production Hours (#)	Product Line
	Sales per Employee ($)	Product Line
	SG&A ($/%)	

FUNCTION	DECISION ROLES	PRIMARY WORK	CONTRIBUTORY	STATUS
Finance				
	Executives	•		
	Managers	•		
	Analysts	•		
	Professionals	•		
Audit				
	Executives			•
	Managers	•		
	Professionals	•		
Customer Service				
	Executives			•
	Analysts		•	
Distribution				
	Executives			•
	Analysts		•	
Marketing				
	Executives			•
	Analysts		•	
Operations / Production				
	Executives			•
	Analysts		•	
Purchasing				
	Executives			•
	Analysts		•	
Product Development				
	Executives			•
	Analysts		•	
Sales				
	Executives			•
	Analysts		•	

Because all the processes are connected to each other at different levels, we are able to check the various plans for reliability on a regular basis, while at the same time adhering to the strategy and taking action quickly when necessary. We have a much better view of where and when deviations from the trends will occur. This is a key indicator of what action we have to take.

Eelco van den Akker, Business Planning Manager, Philips

Cash Flow and Working Capital

Effective collection of accounts receivable fuels better performance. The cost of delay is high; managing the profiles of aging accounts receivable or the days of sales outstanding (DSO) is a key priority for any company. The flip side of the coin is that delaying your own accounts payable is good for cash flow. In both cases, Finance must have insight into customer and supplier preferences to ensure the bottom line does not damage valuable relationships.

Investment analysts scrutinize working capital requirements as one factor in determining financial performance. *Is the business managing its valuable cash resources? How does the ratio of debtors (accounts receivable) to sales or the DSO compare to the industry average? Are stock days increasing, meaning more cash is being diverted to holding stock? Are the accounts payable days increasing?*

Working capital requirements have a direct impact on the market valuation of a business. They are a critical area for Finance to monitor.

GOALS	METRICS	DIMENSIONS
A/R Days (#)	A/P ($)	C/F Lines
Net Cash Flow ($/%)	A/P to Sales (%)	Class
Working Capital Ratio (%)	A/R ($)	Sub-class
	A/R to Sales (%)	Account
	Current Assets ($)	Fiscal Month
	Current Liabilities ($)	Year
	Inventory ($)	Quarter
	Inventory Days (#)	Month
	Inventory to COGS (%)	Organization
	Net Change ($/%)	Division
	Quick Ratio (%)	Department
		Org. Code

FUNCTION	DECISION ROLES	PRIMARY WORK	CONTRIBUTORY	STATUS
Finance				
	Executives	•		
	Managers	•		
	Analysts	•		
	Professionals	•		
Audit				
	Executives			•
	Managers	•		
	Professionals	•		
Human Resources				
	Executives			•
IT / Systems				
	Executives			•
Marketing				
	Executives			•
Operations / Production				
	Executives			•
Product Development				
	Executives			•
Sales				
	Executives			•
	Analysts		•	

Thanks to the colour codes and other alerts provided, our users can easily keep track of outstanding debts. We are also better at credit control, with indicators clearly highlighting our clients' outstanding balances. In addition, the local office managers now have access to tools for monitoring their sales figures. More generally, the whole way that the business is managed has clearly been improved.

Mikael Perhirin, Head of Decision Support and Infocentre Unit, Générale de Protection

Balance Sheet

This decision area balances the financial structure and resources of the business. How much debt, long and short term, can the business safely take on? For shareholders, a higher debt-to-equity ratio means higher rewards and greater risk. A highly leveraged business will generate attractive financial rewards, but if operating profits fall this may jeopardize the company's ability to deliver on interest and debt repayments. The company's financial structure is a balancing act that must be based on business fundamentals. *Are future market conditions likely to be favorable? Are sales increasing or decreasing? Is more cash investment needed in the company's future assets?* Depending on the strategy and future direction, Finance has to accommodate such demands while maximizing returns.

Capital employed—working capital plus fixed assets—and return on capital employed (ROCE) are critical factors that influence how lenders and shareholders value a business. Investors perceive an intensive and high-capital-employed industry as more risky. A high fixed-assets-to-sales ratio is more difficult to manage in an economic downturn, as for example in steel production. ROCE reflects how well the business can convert investment into profit.

Selling the financial attractiveness of the business to new investors is an important Finance function. ROCE is a benchmark that reflects positively or negatively on senior management and Finance. It highlights the importance of managing future investments and having a clear understanding and sense of priority about which investment projects generate better returns. This understanding leads to the next decision area.

GOALS	METRICS	DIMENSIONS
Capital Employed ($)	Actual ($)	Bal. Sheet Lines
Debt-to-Equity Ratio (%)	Assets ($)	Class
ROCE (%)	Debt ($)	Sub-class
	Equity ($)	Fiscal Month
	Fixed Assets ($)	Year
	Fixed Assets/Assets (%)	Quarter
		Month
	Liabilities ($)	Organization
	Liabilities-to-Equity (%)	Division
	Market Value ($)	Department
	Sales/Capital Employed (%)	Org. Code
	Sales/Operating Assets (%)	

FUNCTION	DECISION ROLES	PRIMARY WORK	CONTRIBUTORY	STATUS
Finance				
	Executives	•		
	Managers	•		
	Analysts	•		
	Professionals	•		
Audit				
	Executives			•
	Managers		•	
	Professionals		•	
Marketing				
	Executives			•
Operations / Production				
	Executives			•
Product Development				
	Executives			•
Sales				
	Executives			•

CapEx and Strategic Investments

Since capital expenditure (CapEx) has an impact on ROCE performance, businesses must evaluate and monitor investment decisions carefully. Asset investments can range from minor to strategically significant: from a new computer to a new production plant in a new country. Finance must ensure that CapEx and investment requests don't simply become wish lists.

Finance must establish the basis for prioritizing and justifying capital expenditure. This means coordinating with different function areas. For example, Finance must understand the impact of both yes and no before agreeing to new investments in plant and equipment. *Will the business lose sales if you don't build the plant? Will this action fix product quality problems? Will production costs increase or decrease?*

Mergers and acquisitions represent the strategic dimension of investments. *What are the potential cost savings from combining these two businesses? If the companies serve the same market, will customers be concerned about high supplier dependency and reduce orders? If the businesses are complementary, what is the volume of incremental sales?*

Understanding upside and downside impacts from potential investments is part of the evaluation process. Finance arbitrates such decisions, and requires detailed financial scenarios that forecast investment ROI and payback.

GOALS	METRICS	DIMENSIONS
Investment ($)	Acquisition Profit Growth (%)	Bal. Sheet Lines
NPV ($)	Acquisition Sales Growth (%)	Class
ROI (%)	Assets ($)	Sub-class
	Breakeven Months (#)	Fiscal Month
	Capital Employed Change ($/%)	Year
	Fixed Assets ($)	Quarter
	IRR (%)	Month
	Payback Months (#)	Organization
		Division
		Department
		Org. Code
		Plan/Actual Scenario
		Scenario
		Potential Projects
		R&D Project Type
		Project
		Project
		Project/Program Type
		Project

FUNCTION	DECISION ROLES	PRIMARY WORK	CONTRIBUTORY	STATUS
Finance				
	Executives	•		
	Managers	•		
	Analysts	•		
	Professionals	•		
Audit				
	Executives			•
	Managers	•		
	Professionals	•		
Marketing				
	Executives			•
	Analysts		•	
Operations / Production				
	Executives			•
	Analysts		•	
Product Development				
	Executives			•
	Analysts		•	
Sales				
	Executives			•
	Analysts		•	

Treasury

Moving beyond the strategic finance structure of the balance sheet, there are regular day-to-day liquidity management concerns that require constant attention. Treasury is concerned with the effective management of cash and liquidity, financing, bank relationships, and financial risks. *What are the options for short-term borrowing and cash requirements? Should any surplus cash be placed in the money markets or into a bank account—and if so, at what rate of return and for how long?*

Effectively managing these liquidity options and dealing with bank relationships requires constantly updated information. Having access to current market information and aligning it with future business requirements is the key to effectiveness.

GOALS	METRICS	DIMENSIONS
Borrowing Cost (%)	Shares Issued (#)	Bal. Sheet Lines
Investment Yield (%)	Shares Outstanding (#)	Class
Net Liquidity ($)	Accrued Interest ($)	Sub-class
	Dividend Payments ($/%)	Fiscal Month
	Interest ($/%)	Year
	Investment Risk (#)	Quarter
	Investments ($)	Month
	Loan Balance ($)	Organization
	Net Cash Flow ($)	Division
	Options Outstanding (#)	Department
	Options Paid-Up ($)	Org. Code
	Price Earnings Ratio (#)	
	Repaid ($) – Interest	
	Repaid ($) – Principal	
	U/W Loan Amount ($)	

FUNCTION	DECISION ROLES	PRIMARY WORK	CONTRIBUTORY	STATUS
Finance				
	Executives	•		
	Managers	•		
	Analysts	•		
	Professionals	•		
Audit				
	Executives			•
	Managers	•		
	Professionals	•		

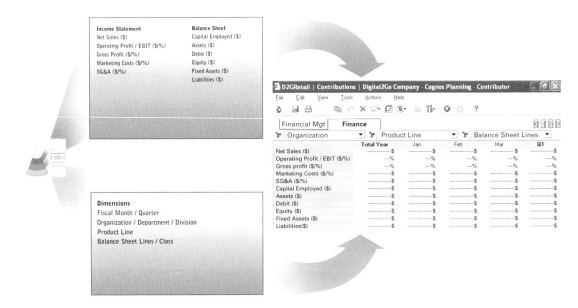

The Income Statement and Balance Sheet decision areas illustrate how the Finance function can monitor its performance, allocate resources, and set plans for future financial targets.

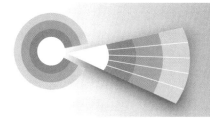

Investment Advisor to the Business

Successful investing is anticipating the anticipations of others.
John Maynard Keynes

These are the facts every Marketing professional understands:

- There are more and more competitors in your market

- Your competitors are constantly changing their business models and value propositions

- Your customers can access massive amounts of information, making them aware of their options, tough bargainers, and fickle

- At the same time, consumers' appetite for products and services continues to change and grow

Your competition and customers will continue to increase in sophistication. Marketing must do so as well if it is to serve the company and help it compete and win. This means its role must evolve.

Marketing must become an *investment advisor* to the business. As that investment advisor, Marketing must define:

- The overall investment strategy—what is sold, where, and to whom

- The strategic path for maximizing return on the company's assets (ROA)

- The cost justification for the operational path required to get there (i.e., support of return on investment (ROI) numbers for scarce marketing dollars)

Marketing must be present in the boardroom, offering business analysis coupled with financial analysis. It must connect the dots among strategic objectives, operational execution, and financial criteria. It can provide the necessary alignment between strategy, operations, and finance.

Marketing must overcome three important barriers to provide this alignment and become an investment advisor. Each barrier underscores the need for information sweet spots, greater accountability, and more integrated decision-making.

Barrier 1: *Defining the "size of prize" has become more complex*

In the days of homogeneous mass markets, companies assessed value based on market share of major product lines, counting on economies of scale in marketing spending and healthy margins to deliver profits. Ten years ago, the challenge evolved from mass markets to defining and improving customer profitability. Companies began to include customer information in their data. Many companies have successfully developed this information sweet spot and now can group customers into meaningful segments.

Today, this trend is evolving as customer requirements and characteristics are divided into smaller and smaller micro-segments, which requires organizations to become responsive to the needs of more and more customer categories.

Size of prize marketing requires the company to do two things well. First, it must pool customers into meaningful micro-segments that are cost-effective to target, acquire, and retain. Second, it must determine the profitability potential of these micro-segments in order to set company priorities. These profit pools allow Marketing to recommend the best investment at product/brand/segment levels. This is of particular relevance when considering different channel strategies: the more detailed the understanding and mapping of micro-segment profits, the more the marketing and sales propositions can be refined.

Barrier 2: *Lack of integrated and enhanced information*

Without appropriate context (*where, who, when*), Marketing can't define or analyze a micro-segment. Without perspective (comparisons), Marketing can't define market share or track trends at this more detailed level.

As an investment advisor, Marketing must merge three core information sources: customer (operational), market (external), and financial. To gain the full value of large volumes of customer data—electronic point-of-sale (EPOS), click-stream data, and feeds from CRM and ERP sources—the information must be structured thoughtfully and integrated cleanly. Marketing's judgments and assessments must be supported by the capability to categorize, group, describe, associate, and otherwise enrich the raw data.

Companies need easy, fast, and seamless access to typical market information such as product category trends, product share, channels, and competitor performance. They also need financial information from the general ledger and planning sources to allocate cost and revenue potential in order to place a value on each profit pool.

Barrier 3: *Number-crunching versus creativity*

Companies create marketing strategies to win customer segments and the associated "prize". Marketing's work now really begins, and it must justify the marketing tactics it proposes, set proper budgets, and demonstrate the strengths and limits of those tactics. Drilling down into greater detail and designing tactics around this information will help satisfy Finance's requirements. In the past, such detailed design has not been the marketing norm, but it is what is required to generate the ROI that Finance wants to see.

However, the right information is not always easy to get. And some departments contend that good ideas are constrained by such financial metrics, stifling the creativity that is the best side of Marketing.

Marketing's traditional creativity should not abandon finding the "big idea", but must expand to include formulating specific actions with a much clearer understanding of *who*, *why*, and *size of prize*. This is not a loss of creativity, simply a means to structure it within a more functional framework.

A Guidance and Early Detection System

As investment advisor, Marketing guides strategic and operational activity, which focuses on the potential of specific markets and how the organization can meet these markets' needs. In this role, Marketing can also be an early detection system for how changes in the market lead to changes in products and services, selling strategies, or even more far-ranging operational elements of the business.

Many marketing metrics are important indicators for a company scorecard. Sudden drops in response rates for traditionally successful marketing efforts could mean competitor pressure, market shifts, and/or revenue trouble down the road. Good marketing departments see the big picture. They notice and interpret trends that are not readily apparent on the front line and provide the business context for what is being sold, or not, and the associated value proposition.

Marketing has the responsibility for defining, understanding, and leading five core areas of the company's decision-making:

- **Market opportunities** ➔ What is the profit opportunity?
- **Competitive positioning** ➔ What are the competitive risks to achieving it?
- **Product life cycle management** ➔ What is our value proposition?
- **Pricing** ➔ What is it worth?
- **Demand generation** ➔ How do we reach and communicate value to customers?

Marketing Opportunities

Making decisions about marketing opportunities is a balancing act between targeting the possibility and managing the probability, while recognizing the absence of certainty. This decision area is fundamentally strategic and concerned with the longer term. It manages the upfront investment and prioritizes the most promising profit pools while dealing with a time lag in results.

Understanding the profit potential in opportunities requires a detailed assessment of pricing, cost to serve, distribution requirements, product quality, resources, employees, and more. The most obvious market opportunities have already been identified, whether by you or the competition. You are looking for the hidden gems buried in the data missed by others. These are the micro-targets that need to be identified, analyzed, and understood.

GOALS	METRICS	DIMENSIONS
Company Share (%)	Market Growth ($)	Fiscal Month
Market Growth Rate (%)	Market Profit ($)	Year
Market Revenue ($)	Market Unit Volume (#)	Quarter
	Profit ($)	Month
	Sales ($)	Industries
	Unit Volume Sales (#)	SIC 2-Digit
		SIC 4-Digit
		Marketing Areas
		Region
		Area
		Marketing Segment
		Market Segment
		Micro-Segment
		Product Brand
		Product Line
		Brand
		Sales Organization
		Sales Region
		Sales Territory
		Org. Code

FUNCTION	DECISION ROLES	PRIMARY WORK	CONTRIBUTORY	STATUS
Marketing				
	Executives	•		
	Managers	•		
	Analysts	•		
	Professionals	•		
Product Development				
	Executives			•
	Analysts		•	
Sales				
	Executives			•
	Managers		•	
	Analysts		•	
Finance				
	Executives			•
	Analysts		•	

Competitive Positioning

Effective competitive positioning means truly understanding what you offer as products and/or services to the segments you target, and how they compare with those of other suppliers. As an investment advisor, Marketing must clearly define the business and competitive proposition: *In which market segments are you competing, and with what products and services?*

Marketing must define and invest in specific information sweet spots that give it insight into how its customer selection criteria compare to those of its competitors. Marketing must understand the customer-relevant differentiators in its offerings and the life span of those differentiators based on, for example, how difficult they are to copy. It also needs to understand the pricing implications of this information.

- Are our price points below or above those of key competitors, and by how much?

- If below, is this sustainable given our cost profile, or is cost a future threat?

- What premium will customers pay for value-added propositions?

GOALS	METRICS	DIMENSIONS
Competitor Growth (%)	Competitor Price Change ($)	Competitor
Competitor Price Change (%)	Competitor Sales ($)	Competitor Type
Competitor Share (%)	Market Growth ($)	Competitor Company
	Market Profit ($)	Fiscal Month
	Market Revenue ($)	Year
	Sales ($)	Quarter
		Month
		Industries
		SIC 2-Digit
		SIC 4-Digit
		Marketing Areas
		Region
		Area
		Marketing Segment
		Market Segment
		Micro-Segment
		Product Brand
		Product Line
		Brand
		Sales Organization
		Sales Region
		Sales Territory
		Org. Code

FUNCTION	DECISION ROLES	PRIMARY WORK	CONTRIBUTORY	STATUS
Marketing				
	Executives	•		
	Managers	•		
	Analysts	•		
	Professionals	•		
Sales				
	Executives			•
	Managers		•	
	Analysts	•		
	Professionals		•	
Product Development				
	Executives			•
	Analysts		•	

Product Life Cycle Management

Products are born, grow, and die. Marketing organizations must manage the product life cycle and maximize the return at every stage by adapting or retiring unprofitable products and introducing new ones. Life cycles vary significantly between industries and market segments. For example, computer technology evolves over a 12-month cycle; cars have a three- to five-year cycle. This pace of innovation (which is subject to sudden change) sets the context in which management needs to bring "new news" to your markets. New news fuels the marketing machinery, a significant way to excite and capture customer mindshare. It is also tied to financial performance, as product innovation may point to future earnings.

Innovation may mean small or significant changes to existing products as well as the introduction of completely new products. For example, based on its understanding of existing and new segments, Marketing can drive changes in packaging and pricing to target new opportunities. These changes can be achieved in the short term or the long term and are part of Marketing's role in defining profitability targets and predictions.

Companies have portfolios of products/services, each in its own stage of the product life cycle. The classic practice of defining products/services as stars, cash cows, and dogs forces product review with dimensions of time, profitability, and competitive advantage. Product life cycle management continues the process of competitive positioning and market opportunity definition. Marketing identifies new opportunities, is aware of the competitive landscape, and then looks into what products and services will best do the job.

Marketing should understand what proportion of existing sales comes from new products and compare this percentage with that of competitors. This measure helps the organization judge the impact of investing more or less in innovation. As an investment advisor, Marketing is in a position to counsel the company on how to forecast changes in market share if the company does not introduce new products in a given time period. In-depth analysis allows the company to segment products by their various life cycles and corresponding expectations, so the company can plan new product introductions.

GOALS	METRICS	DIMENSIONS
New Product Growth (%)	Brand Equity Score (#)	Fiscal Month
New Product Share (%)	Market Growth ($)	Year
Relative New Product Share (%)	Net Price ($)	Quarter
	New Competitor Product Sales ($)	Month
	New Competitor Product Share (%)	Marketing Areas
	New Product Growth ($)	Region
	New Product Profit ($)	Area
	New Product Sales ($)	Marketing Segment
	New Products Developed (#)	Market Segment
	Sales Revenue ($)	Micro-Segment
		Product SKU
		Product Line
		Brand
		SKU
		Time-in-Market Range
		Range

FUNCTION	DECISION ROLES	PRIMARY WORK	CONTRIBUTORY	STATUS
Finance				
	Executives			•
	Analysts		•	
Marketing				
	Executives	•		
	Analysts	•		
Operations / Production				
	Executives			•
	Analysts		•	
Purchasing				
	Executives			•
	Analysts		•	
Product Development				
	Executives			•
	Analysts		•	
Sales				
	Executives			•
	Analysts		•	

Pricing

Companies once defined their product proposition broadly to cast the widest net possible in homogeneous mass markets. The downside of this practice was that as a product became a general commodity, it became subject to price sensitivity. Smart marketers today see micro-segment markets not as a challenge, but as an opportunity to define smaller, more customized offerings that are less price-sensitive. The more your product proposition is tailored to solve a specific customer's problem, the easier it is to protect your price and margin.

Tailoring the product proposition requires more detailed information. Simple reports from transactional systems can provide enough information to support homogeneous mass-marketing strategies. Targeting micro-segments means modeling price implications and tracking results at many levels.

- What product and service bundling opportunities are possible for given market segments and customers?

- Does the product portfolio offer a combined value and convenience advantage that can be priced tactically?

- What impact will an increase/decrease in price have upon volumes (a measure of price elasticity)?

- To what extent should pricing be used as a defensive versus aggressive tool, and what are the relative cost benefits? For example, where a business has only a small market share, does it pay to be aggressive in its competitor's back yard?

Setting prices based on well-thought-out models is one thing, but companies also must monitor how flexible local offices and sales teams need to be. Centralized pricing ensures margin stability, but can be counterproductive in a fast-moving, competitive situation. As a compromise, companies typically offer pricing guidelines and a pricing floor. This lets local sales reps respond to competitive pressures but protects the business from dangerously low price levels. Good marketing systems monitor this data to test the validity of pricing assumptions, as well as to gain early warning of competitor attacks on pricing.

Particularly useful are product-specific analyses—according to customer segment, product group, or packaging type. This allows the company to focus on units that best suit the market whilst at the same time providing the most attractive option to the company in terms of cost.

Andreas Speck, Head of Information Management, Kotányi GmbH

Well-designed sales incentives can help avoid price erosion, but experience shows that these can also encourage unintended behaviors. Developing sales incentives without implementing a reporting system on those incentives is a recipe for wasting money. The ability to manage pricing guidelines while offering local sales reps the flexibility they require depends on the use of information from business intelligence and planning tools.

GOALS	METRICS	DIMENSIONS
Price Change (%)	Average Price ($)	Billing Customer
Price Segment Growth (%)	Discount ($)	Industry Group
Price Segment Share (%)	Discount Spread (%)	Industry
	List Price ($)	Category
	Net Price ($)	Customer Name
	Price Change ($)	Competitor
	Price Elasticity Factor	Competitor Type
	Price Segment Sales ($)	Competitor Company
	Price Segment Value ($)	Customer Sales Rel. Status
	Sales ($)	Status
	Unit Volume Sales (#)	Fiscal Month
		Year
		Quarter
		Month
		Marketing Areas
		Region
		Area
		Marketing Segment
		Market Segment
		Micro-Segment
		Product Brand
		Product Line
		Brand
		Sales Organization
		Sales Region
		Sales Territory
		Org. Code

FUNCTION	DECISION ROLES	PRIMARY WORK	CONTRIBUTORY	STATUS
Marketing				
	Executives	•		
	Managers	•		
	Analysts	•		
	Professionals	•		
Sales				
	Executives			•
	Analysts		•	
Finance				
	Executives			•
	Analysts		•	
Product Development				
	Executives			•
	Analysts		•	
Operations / Production				
	Executives			•
	Analysts		•	
Customer Schedule				
	Executives			•
	Analysts		•	

Demand Generation

Driving demand is where Marketing rubber hits the road. All of Marketing's strategic thinking and counseling about micro-segments, profit potential, the offer, and competitive pressures comes to life in advertising, promotions, online efforts, public relations, and events.

Marketing manages its tactical performance by analyzing promotions, communications, marketing campaigns, below-the-line support, internal resourcing, response rates, and cost per response. At the same time, Marketing must understand whether or not the company is acquiring the right customers for the ideal future portfolio. This is key to understanding the results of a micro-segment marketing effort.

Improving Marketing tactics is not simply about designing more detailed and specific activities; it also means understanding what elements work better than others. Marketing must understand the health and vitality of its various decision areas, including pricing, promotions, packaging changes, and consumer communications. *What provokes a greater response? At what cost?* With a wide variety of options for online, direct response, and traditional advertising, Marketing needs to know which tools work best for which groups.

GOALS	METRICS	DIMENSIONS
Baseline Sales ($)	Brand Equity Score (#)	Fiscal Month
Incremental Sales ($)	Marketing Campaigns (#)	Year
Promotions ROI (%)	Marketing Spend ($)	Quarter
	Marketing Spend/Lead ($)	Month
	Non-Promoted Margin (%)	Marketing Areas
	Non-Promoted Sales ($)	Region
	Promoted Margin (%)	Area
	Promoted Profit ($)	Marketing Method
	Promoted Sales ($)	Marketing Method
	Qualified Leads (#)	Marketing Segment
	Sales on Promotion (%)	Market Segment
		Micro-Segment
		Marketing Campaign Projects
		Marketing Campaign Type
		Marketing Campaign
		Product Line
		Product Line
		Sales Organization
		Sales Region
		Sales Territory
		Org. Code
		Weeks on Promotion

FUNCTION	DECISION ROLES	PRIMARY WORK	CONTRIBUTORY	STATUS
Marketing				
	Executives	•		
	Managers	•		
	Analysts	•		
	Professionals	•		
Sales				
	Executives			•
	Managers		•	
	Professionals		•	
Customer Service				
	Executives			•
	Analysts		•	
Finance				
	Executives			•
	Analysts		•	

Understanding and analyzing this information is key to alignment and accountability. Driving demand requires close alignment with Sales, and Marketing tactical teams continually fine-tune their aim and selection of tactical "arrows" until they hit the bull's-eye.

Sales managers can implement the plans as agreed with customers, and promotions can be planned at both market and consumer level. Furthermore, there is a much greater understanding of the impact that developments have on the profitability of products.

Eelco van den Akker, Business Planning Manager, Philips

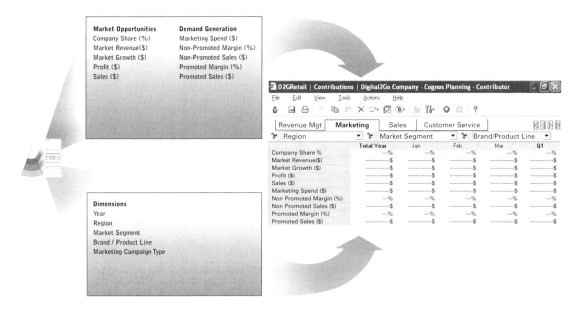

The Marketing Opportunities and Demand Generation decision areas illustrate how the Marketing function can monitor its performance, allocate resources, and set plans for future financial targets.

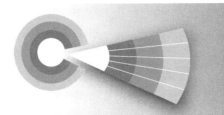

Your Business Accelerator

Things may come to those who wait, but only things left by those who hustle.
Abraham Lincoln

Not Enough Time, Not Fast Enough

Customers are increasingly educated and competent. To close a sale, reps must be able to react, adjust, and satisfy customer demands on the spot. Understanding customer needs and credibility in offering a solution are prerequisites for even being in the running. New customer demands mean sales conversations have become far more complex, demanding a wider range of product knowledge, sales techniques, customer insights, and company-wide awareness. And the customer expects an immediate response. This is the key challenge facing today's sales rep: how to balance the need for immediate customer response with gaining the right information to satisfy the customer and close the sale.

The ability to close deals efficiently and the knowledge needed to invest your time in the right customers are critical factors driving your company's success. Both depend on a timely, two-way flow of information. Accurate and speedy information can help improve sales results and reduce selling costs. Information flowing through Sales can affect every other department in the company: for example, high demand forecasts drive greater future production. The slower the two-way flow of information, the less responsive the organization.

This viewpoint brings together the three core insights in this book (see Introduction). Sales has clear accountability for results, requires information sweet spots, and thrives on the most integrated decision-making capabilities. A sales force with the right information, at the right time, driven by the right incentives, is formidable. Unfortunately, many Sales departments do not optimize time and speed of execution due to three barriers.

Barrier 1: *You don't set sales targets and allocate effort based on maximizing overall contribution*

How you measure performance and set compensation drives how Sales allocates its time. If you define sales targets in terms of potential profit and contribution, Sales will invest time where it maximizes sustainable company returns. Customer relationships that secure today's orders and tomorrow's sales are a strong competitive advantage. If focusing Sales on customer and product profitability isn't a new thought, and it's not difficult to see the benefits—why is it still rare in terms of implementation?

There are several reasons. In some cases, integrated profitability information is unavailable or is too sensitive to distribute. Determining how to allocate costs may be complex or politically charged. More frequently, the company's focus on short-term revenue means Sales does not have or need a perspective on long-term customer contributions. As a result, it neglects to measure cross-sell and up-sell revenue paths or the estimated lifetime value of a customer.

The customer's potential lifetime value is not static: it changes over time. A good Sales professional can positively affect the change. Effecting positive change requires that reps understand:

- The cost benefit of maintaining versus acquiring customers
- Relative weighting of various opportunities based on the "cost" of expected effort
- Longer-term planning as opposed to a single sales opportunity
- A multi-tiered portfolio approach to opportunities

Without these sweet spots, your time may be poorly invested. Or worse, you won't know if it is or isn't.

Barrier 2: *There is no two-way clearinghouse for the right information at the right time*

Procurement departments are more precisely benchmarked and more subject to internal scrutiny. These departments expect reliable company-to-company relationships, where vendors are business advisors and valued solutions experts. Sales, too, is becoming more and more about information rather than just products and relationships.

However, turning sales professionals into experts on every topic is not the answer. There is simply too much customer information required to process, distill, and communicate for reps to be fully educated on every possible buying scenario. Instead, Sales needs to become an efficient clearinghouse of the right information at the right time.

What's missing in most companies is an effective two-way flow of "smart facts" between the customer and the company. Smart facts are focused information packages about customer needs and challenges, company advantages, and important interaction points between both entities.

The two-way nature of this information is critical. The entire organization (Marketing and Product Development in particular) needs customer insights into what works, what doesn't, and what is of greatest importance. Without this, your response to important concerns is impeded, and you won't understand the customer perspective, which is necessary for sustainable relationships.

Smart facts let Sales:

- Build on customer success stories and best practices

- Link understood company values to what the customer requires

- Proactively deal with issues between the customer and company (such as late deliveries, etc.) and stay on top of the account

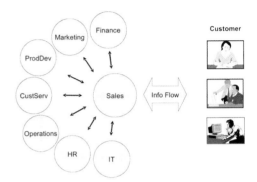

Sales: two-way clearinghouse of smart, fast facts

Sales reps—your front line with customers—are at a disadvantage when trying to build reliable company-to-company relationships and loyalty if you do not provide them with these smart facts in a timely fashion.

Barrier 3: *You don't measure the underlying drivers of sales effectiveness*

What type of input drives the most output, as measured by sales success? This is rarely evaluated or understood, and yet it is one of the most critical areas for a company to master.

Lead generation, customer preparation, sales calls, and collateral material are all familiar tactics of the sales process. The missed opportunity comes from not tracking what expectations were set around these tactics and not monitoring what actually happens. Despite significant investments in sales force automation and customer relationship management systems, companies miss this opportunity when they see setting targets as a complicated planning exercise or when it conflicts with a company bias to rely more on intuition.

The choice doesn't have to be either/or. Experience and intuition can guide the initial tactical choices and outcome expectations—but monitoring these outcomes lets you make informed decisions to improve your results. Your goal is to increase sales productivity and adjust tactics when something doesn't work. Without set expectations and a means to monitor the underlying drivers of sales effectiveness, you will likely suffer both higher selling costs and missed sales targets.

Continuous Accelerated Realignment

The five decision areas described below can improve the speed of sales execution and enable a more effective use of time. They rely on the two-way flow of vital information between customers and company. This sharing of information can accelerate the speed of adjustments and realignments of product, market, message, service, and other elements of the business.

Decision areas in Sales:

- **Sales results** → What is driving sales performance?
- **Customer/product profitability** → What is driving contribution performance?
- **Sales tactics** → What is driving sales effectiveness?
- **Sales pipeline** → What is driving the sales pipeline?
- **Sales plan variance** → What is driving the sales plan?

The order of these decision areas reflects a logical flow of analysis and action. They start with understanding where Sales is achieving its results, first in terms of overall sales performance and then in terms of net contribution. This is followed by drilling deeper into how Sales is using its time and to what effect. Finally, the insights gained are applied to revising the planning and forecasting process. In this way, Sales can drive a continuous and accelerated re-examination and realignment of the organization. This cycle is anchored by the organization's strategic objectives (profitability and net contribution) and incorporates frontline realities for an accurate view of Sales performance.

Sales Results

Sales results are one of the most basic and important information sweet spots. They are one of the two foundations of Sales management, the other being Sales planning. They provide a consistent overview of actual revenue across the five basic components of the business—product, customer, territory, channel, and time.

Accurate understanding of these components suggests why results diverge from expectations. *Are sales trending down in certain territories? Is this consistent across all products, channels, sales reps, and customers?*

Sales results should not be confined to managerial levels but should be shared at various levels of the organization. You can empower frontline sales reps with appropriately packaged analytic information, adapted for individual reps with specific product portfolios in specific territories.

Beyond immediate operational analysis, sales results let you recognize broader performance patterns to see if strategies and management objectives are on track and still making sense. With a consistent flow of information over time, you can make more strategic comparisons, interpretations, and adjustments. For example, if sales are flat in the premium customer segment, you need to know: *Is this a tactical problem or a strategic one—i.e., should this lead to a full re-evaluation of the company's future in the premium segment? Are significant resource investments necessary to revive this segment? Has the product proposition been outflanked by the competition?* These questions are part of an accurate assessment of sales results.

Sales results information also connects time spent, level of responsibility, strategic decision-making, and operational activities. If you identify a weakness in a commodity segment of the market, the business has a number of time-related options to deal with it. A drop in such sales in the short term may cause serious competitive damage, leading to long-term difficulties. The short-term solution might be a series of sales push activities, such as more promotions and discounts. Given the impact of this on margin, however, management may choose to look at the overall product portfolio to find opportunities to cut product costs. This may require long-term strategic decisions at the highest level of the organization involving Marketing, Product Development, Operations, and Finance. Sales results are one of the main contributors of information for this decision. The speed and accuracy with which Sales provides this information to the company is critical. More of this dynamic will be covered in the Executive Management chapter.

SALES RESULTS

GOALS	METRICS	DIMENSIONS	
New Customer Sales ($)	Avg. Sales per Order ($)	Billing Customer	Product SKU
Sales Growth (%)	Avg. Units per Order (#)	Industry Group	Product Line
Sales Order ($)	Credit Balance ($)	Industry	Brand
	Credit Limit ($)	Category	SKU
	Customers (#)	Customer Name	Sales Channel Partners
	Lost Customer Count (#)	Customer Location	Sales Channel Type
	New Customer Count (#)	Region	Sales Partner
	New Product Sales ($)	State/Province	Sales Organization
	Sales Order Count (#)	County	Sales Region
	Units Ordered (#)	Postal Code/Zip Code	Sales Territory
		Fiscal Week	Org. Code
		Fiscal Year	Ship-To Location
		Quarter	Region
		Month	State/Province
		Week	County
		Market Segment	City
		Market Segment	Postal Code/Zip Code
		Micro-Segment	

FUNCTION	DECISION ROLES	PRIMARY WORK	CONTRIBUTORY	STATUS
Marketing				
	Executives			•
	Managers		•	
	Analysts		•	
	Professionals		•	
Sales				
	Executives	•		
	Managers	•		
	Analysts	•		
	Professionals	•		
Audit				
	Executives			•
	Managers	•		
	Professionals	•		
Finance				
	Executives			•
	Analysts		•	
Customer Service				
	Executives		•	
	Analysts		•	
Operations / Production				
	Executives			•
Product Development				
	Executives			•
	Analysts		•	
Customer Service				
	Executives	•		
	Analysts	•		

Planning is pointless if it isn't translated into action plans that are actually delivered and analysed. At the same time, there's no point in automating your sales force if you can't direct them towards achieving the relevant goals.

Vincent Meunier, Information Systems Director, Pernod

Customer/Product Profitability

The key to this decision area is recognizing which customers and products are making the largest contributions. A basic gross profit view is possible using a "sales minus discounts and standard costs" formula for customers and products. Once this is calculated, you can develop more complex views by allocating direct costs using certain drivers to determine either effort or activity plus related costs. This allows you to recognize net profit at the relationship and product levels by applying expense and allocation formulas. Using a phased approach when moving from gross to net profit enables learning by successive iterations, and the benefit of gaining wins and proof of value before tackling more complex cost allocations. The sales force must adopt the profit goals and work with the rest of the organization on achieving them.

Understanding customer lifetime profitability is vital to a business. It focuses the organization on the value of the long-term customer. Customer/product profitability is a powerful tool that is used at senior levels of marketing and corporate strategy. The sensitivity of this information dictates that it cannot be widely distributed, but by indexing some of this information for the sales force, you ensure Sales understands its profit priorities and is ready to put that knowledge into action.

GOALS	METRICS	DIMENSIONS	
Average Customer Profit ($)	Cost ($)	Billing Customer	Market Segment
	Customer Acquisition Cost ($)	Industry Group	Market Segment
Lifetime Profit ($)	Customer Retention Cost ($)	Industry	Micro-Segment
Net Profit ($)	Customers (#)	Category	Organization
	Discount ($)	Customer Name	Division
	Gross Profit ($/%)	Customer Location	Department
	Net Sales ($)	Region	Org. Code
	Sales Revenue ($)	State/Province	Product SKU
	Units Sold (#)	County	Product Line
		Postal Code/Zip Code	Brand
		Fiscal Month	SKU
		Year	Sales Channel / Partners
		Quarter	Sales Channel Type
		Month	Sales Partner

FUNCTION	DECISION ROLES	PRIMARY WORK	CONTRIBUTORY	STATUS
Finance				
	Executives			•
	Managers		•	
	Analysts	•		
	Professionals		•	
Sales				
	Executives	•		
	Analysts	•		
Marketing				
	Executives			•
	Analysts		•	
IT / Systems				
	Executives			•
	Analysts		•	
Product Development				
	Executives			•
	Analysts		•	
Customer Service				
	Analysts		•	
Distribution				
	Analysts		•	
Human Resources				
	Analysts		•	
Operations / Production				
	Analysts		•	
Purchasing				
	Analysts		•	

The development and profitability of each product group can be analyzed separately. The same goes for strategic analyses of customer segments. In other words, the management of the holding company can examine the profitability figures for each individual product group or customer segment and link these groups or segments together, an efficient way to obtain the management information it needs.

Michael-Hagen Weese, Controller and Project Leader, Raiffeisen International Bank-Holding AG

Sales Tactics

This decision area evaluates the sales process to determine which activities and mechanics are most effective. The key is to understand what resources, activities, and tools you need to achieve targets for specific channels and accounts. This decision area continually monitors and reviews the *what* (resources) versus the *how* (mechanics).

The *what* includes understanding the following: *How many prospects are available for sales visits? How many cold and warm calls do you make? How much time is spent on research? How much time is spent with existing customers versus time with new customers? What is the proportion of direct sales to indirect sales?* You require insight into all these areas to optimize time and resources.

The *how* includes understanding how the cost and time spent on activities like pricing, promotions, demonstrations, catalogs, leaflets, and free samples will drive sales.

By combining these two viewpoints, Sales departments are able to guide greater sales effectiveness.

Sales tactics are a direct extension of the Sales performance decision area. You need a structured and coordinated understanding of sales tactics to manage your customers and sales effort effectively. This information must be accessible by your frontline Sales reps to direct their efforts and help them learn from the success of others.

GOALS	METRICS	DIMENSIONS
Average Selling Price ($)	Avg. Sales Hrs/Inquiry (#)	Billing Customer
Direct Cost ($)	Close Days (#)	Industry Group
Discount (%)	Cost per Order ($)	Industry
Sales Calls (#)	Customers (#)	Category
	Discount (%)	Customer Name
	Inactive Customers (#)	Credit Limit Range
	Inquiries ($)	Range
	Inquiry Count (#)	Customer Location
	Inquiry S/O Conversion (%)	Region
	Lost Business Count (#)	State/Province
	Net Price ($)	County
	Quoted ($)	Postal Code/Zip Code
	Rep T&E ($)	Fiscal Week
	Sales Orders ($)	Fiscal Year
	Sales Order Count (#)	Quarter
	Sales Prospect Rating Score	Month
	Sales Rep Days (#)	Week
	Units Quoted (#)	Market Segment
		Market Segment
		Micro-Segment
		Product Brand
		Product Line
		Brand
		Sales Organization
		Sales Region
		Sales Territory
		Org. Code
		Sales Time Priority Rating
		Priority Rating

FUNCTION	DECISION ROLES	PRIMARY WORK	CONTRIBUTORY	STATUS
Sales				
	Executives	•		
	Managers	•		
	Analysts	•		
	Professionals	•		
Finance				
	Executives			•
	Analysts		•	
Marketing				
	Executives			•
	Analysts		•	

We have a comprehensive view of customer behavior—which products they buy, how they pay, whether they are likely to switch, etc. This will yield large financial rewards, since we know precisely which customers are the most valuable to us and how we can best adapt our activities to satisfy them.

Ton van den Dungen, Manager, Business Intelligence and Control, ENECO Energie

Sales Pipeline

This is more than a sales forecast; it is an opportunity to see into your company's future and change it. The Sales pipeline is critical as an early warning system of future opportunities, growth, and problem areas.

By defining and monitoring the phases of the sales pipeline, you can derive metrics that let you establish, follow, and manage business trends. Your pipeline intelligence can become even more sophisticated by looking at details such as new versus existing customers, territories, product groups, markets, and more.

GOALS	METRICS	DIMENSIONS	
Pipeline Ratio (%)	Active Customers (#)	Billing Customer	Market Segment
Pipeline Revenue ($)	Avg. Sales per Order ($)	Industry Group	Market Segment
Sales Order Conversion (%)	Cancelled Order Count (#)	Industry	Micro-Segment
	Inactive Customers (#)	Category	Sales Channel / Partners
	Inquiries ($)	Customer Name	Sales Channel Type
	Inquiry Count (#)	Contracted Pay't Time	Sales Partner
	Inquiry/Quote Lead Days (#)	Range	Sales Organization
	Lost Business Count (#)	Fiscal Week	Sales Region
	New/Lost Customer Ratio (%)	Fiscal Year	Sales Territory
	New Customer Count (#)	Quarter	Org. Code
	S/O Quotes (#)	Month	Ship-To Location
	Sales Order ($)	Week	Region
	Sales Order Count (#)	Inquiry – S/O Status	State/Province
		Inquiry S/O Status	County
		Mfg. Product Component	City
		Product Line	Postal Code/Zip Code
		SKU	
		Component	

Each metric suggests useful business questions that can lead to positive functional change: *Why do only 10 percent of customer visits lead to inquiries? How does this compare with the competition's experience? What would it take to increase this ratio to 20 percent (for example, a lower list price)? Why are some orders lost?*

FUNCTION	DECISION ROLES	PRIMARY WORK	CONTRIBUTORY	STATUS
Sales				
	Executives	•		
	Managers	•		
	Analysts	•		
	Professionals	•		
Customer Service				
	Executives			•
	Analysts		•	
Distribution				
	Executives			•
	Analysts		•	
Operations / Production				
	Executives		•	
	Analysts		•	
Purchasing				
	Executives			•
	Analysts		•	

The sales pipeline should tie into operations, typically to production and purchasing plans. The more predictive and accurate the sales plan is in terms of product, the more efficiently production can manage its processes, reduce changes to production schedules that are due to selling out of products, and stop expensive reactive purchases due to short-term shortages.

Thanks to this solution, company executives can plan out sales, costs, and deployment of staff, modify these on an ongoing basis, and use these plans to identify strategic, tactical, and operational measures.

Marina Glodzei, Project Manager BI Applications, Coloplast GmbH

Sales Plan Variance

Sales planning is a control mechanism, tightly linked to the budgeting and planning process. But it is also a way to manage change and understand the ebb and flow of your business. Unfortunately, the control side tends to dominate.

A top-down budgeting process, where corporate objectives must be achieved (e.g., double-digit revenue growth), emphasizes planning over the actual situation. This leads to companies identifying and plugging revenue gaps with short-term revenue solutions, usually at the expense of long-term strategy—milking the future to get results today.

More useful revenue plans work from the bottom up. Alignment and accountability must be organizational values. Every department provides feedback on revenue objectives, markets, customers, channels, and products. Iterations of this process may be needed to fit with top-down corporate objectives, but it allows individuals across the organization to own their numbers and be fully accountable.

When the entire business is engaged in monitoring under/overperformance, frontline levels of the organization can answer questions regarding the *where* and *why* of existing revenue targets. The sales rep responsible for a missed customer revenue target can explain the *why* and suggest ways to correct the gap.

GOALS	METRICS	DIMENSIONS
Sales Order ($)	Avg. Sales per Order ($)	Fiscal Month
Sales Plan ($/%)	New Customer Sales ($)	Year
	New Product Sales ($)	Quarter
	Sales Growth Rate (%)	Month
	Units Ordered (#)	Forecast Scenario (Plan/Actual/Forecast)
	Units Sold (#)	Scenario
		Market Segment
		Market Segment
		Micro-Segment
		Product Line
		Product Line
		Sales Channel Partners
		Sales Channel Type
		Sales Partner
		Sales Organization
		Sales Region
		Sales Territory
		Org. Code

FUNCTION	DECISION ROLES	PRIMARY WORK	CONTRIBUTORY	STATUS
Finance				
	Executives	•		
	Managers	•		
	Analysts	•		
	Professionals	•		
Audit				
	Executives			•
	Managers	•		
	Professionals	•		
Customer Service				
	Executives			•
	Analysts		•	
Finance				
	Executives			•
	Analysts		•	
Operations / Production				
	Executives			•
	Analysts		•	
Purchasing				
	Executives			•
	Analysts		•	

We believe that best practice planning should not be in the hands of a small group and we are committed to changing this at Ricoh to make planning more participative and collaborative.

Nur Miah, Senior Business Analyst, Ricoh

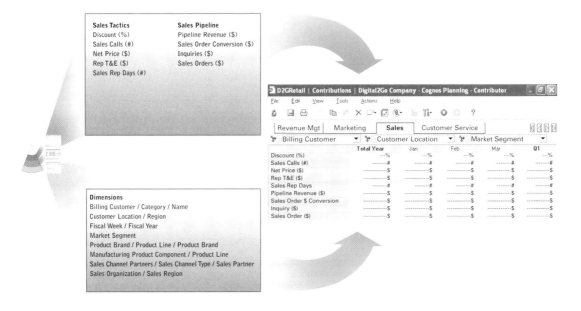

The Sales Tactics and Sales Pipeline decision areas illustrate how the Sales function can monitor its performance, allocate resources, and set plans for future financial targets.

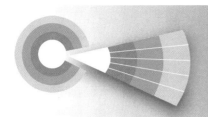
The Risk/Reward Barometer of the Company's Value Proposition

There is only one boss. The customer. And he can fire everybody in the company from the chairman on down, simply by spending his money somewhere else.
Sam Walton

The rewards of good customer experience are straightforward: a satisfied customer is more likely to be loyal and generate more repeat business. There are related benefits:

- Customer retention is far cheaper than customer acquisition.

- A loyal customer is a strong competitive advantage.

- A satisfied customer can become "part of the team", helping to sell your value internally and even identify cross-sell and up-sell opportunities, as well as generate word-of-mouth referrals.

- Such customers are also a great source of new product ideas, competitive intelligence, and industry credibility.

Taken as a whole, the benefits of achieving great customer satisfaction are like a multi-tiered annuity stream. Wall Street rewards annuities because they reduce uncertainty and volatility.

The risks of poor customer service are greater and more insidious because they are less visible. For every unhappy customer you hear from, there are countless more. Negative word of mouth can damage years of good reputation and ripple through countless prospects who never become customers. Ultimately, unhappy customers become lower sales for you and higher market share for your competitor.

Customer Service is both an advocate for the customer within the company, and an advocate for the company with the customer. It generates unique insight into the customer experience, providing an outside view on the company value proposition.

However, many companies pay little more than lip service to customer relationships. They view Customer Service as a necessary expense, as opposed to a critical barometer of the company's sustainable value.

Three significant barriers must be overcome to change this view.

Barrier 1: *Insufficient visibility of the risks to customer loyalty uncovered by Customer Service*

Customer service can be thankless and hectic. Picture a room full of service representatives juggling calls from frustrated customers, often in outsourced and offshore call centers. In such a volume-driven environment, it is difficult to determine the context and pattern of the calls received.

Some companies have made major investments in customer relationship management, specifically in call center software. While these technologies make call centers more efficient, they generate vast amounts of transaction detail that can obscure meaningful patterns and root causes.

Finding patterns in problems such as delivery delays, information requests, complaints, and claims can lead to proactive solutions. Categorizing the types of complaints by quality, order error, response time, and resolution time can reduce service costs and identify the causes of dissatisfaction. Informed companies can address problems at the source and understand the pattern and context of the calls they receive.

Even when you can't eliminate the root cause, better categorization of issues can speed up the time taken to resolve problems. Timely responsiveness can salvage many frustrated customer relationships. As one executive of a major airline said: "Customers don't expect you to be perfect. They do expect you to fix things when they go wrong." Achieving this requires that problems and their causes be grouped and studied so that effective action can be taken.

Barrier 2: *Poor visibility of the benefits of a good customer experience, especially when grouped by who and how*

While many companies know how much they save by reducing customer service, few can project the cost of lower service levels. In particular, you need to understand how customer service levels affect your key and most profitable customer segments. If you don't, you may understate—or overstate—the risk. Overstating the risk leads to an inefficient allocation of resources, which reinforces the view that Customer Service is an expense. Understating the risk can be even worse, leading to the loss of your most valuable customers—the ones your strategy counts on—and the marketing impact of negative word of mouth on other customers.

Good Customer Service departments take into account the absolute and relative lifetime revenue of customer segments, and prioritize service efforts for high-reward customers. Beyond direct future benefits, you may also segment strategic customers that represent new markets or product champions. The key is to segment Customer Service issues by *who*—the customers that matter most to your current and future bottom line.

Once companies understand which customer segments are most important, they must gain insight into how the relationship works. In complex customer-company interactions (for example, with your doctor, or with technology and software vendors) the relationship depends on expertise. This is a clear market differentiator. If the customer-company interaction is more basic (for example, with a department store), then the day-to-day efficiency of the relationship becomes more important for both parties.

Segmenting customer relationship channel interaction helps to clearly define the relative value of great service. When you include the relative value of the customer, you have a useful framework to maximize the rewards of service for you and the customer. For example, if your expertise in complex channels is a differentiator, you may want to offer it free to high-value customers in return for greater loyalty. At the same time, you may want to charge low-value customers extra for this service.

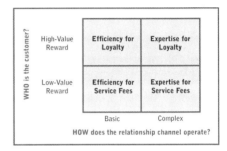

Whatever metrics you choose, you must align them with what the customer perceives as important. *Does the customer value quality above price? Is order accuracy more important than speed in delivery? What are acceptable lead times? Customers may always want delivery yesterday, but are shorter lead times worth a premium?* Understanding the relative importance of such elements will make customer service monitoring more relevant.

Barrier 3: *The absence of a customer advocate and direct accountability*

Ideally, your entire organization has common customer service performance goals. You should back up this alignment with accountability and incentives, especially when the different drivers of those goals span different functions. The lack of these is a barrier to achieving better customer service.

Overcoming this barrier requires clear, credible, and aligned customer service metrics—and the political will and organizational culture to rely on them for tough decisions. *Do you incur higher costs in the short term to secure long-term customer loyalty?* Only companies that understand the risks and rewards of customer service can make informed decisions on such questions.

Customer Service has a key role in generating and sharing this information. Beyond being the handling agent, it can become an effective customer advocate to other departments, and an expert on customer performance metrics and their drivers. It has to understand the problems and the operational solutions. Most important, Customer Service must effectively communicate these metrics to the rest of the organization so that other departments can resolve the root causes of customer experience issues.

This works both ways. Not only must Customer Service bring in other functions to resolve problems, it should offer useful information in return. For example, trends in the type of complaints or problems can suggest quality improvements and operational efficiencies in production. Forewarning a sales rep about service issues before that rep meets with the customer allows Sales to craft an appropriate message and offer assistance. Mutual cooperation like this demonstrates the responsiveness of the organization and can salvage troubled relationships.

Excellence in Customer Experience

The four decision areas described below equip Customer Service with the critical risk and reward information they need to be more effective customer advocates, bringing excellence to the customer experience.

Decision areas in Customer Service:

- **On-time delivery** ➔ What is driving delivery performance?

- **Information, complaints, and claims** ➔ What is driving responsiveness?

- **Service benchmarks** ➔ What is driving service levels?

- **Service value** ➔ What is driving the service cost and benefit?

The sequence of these decision areas provides a logical flow of analysis and action, starting with understanding the primary drivers of risk. First and foremost, did you deliver on time what the customer purchased? Customers do not easily forgive failures in this area; such mistakes therefore carry the greatest risk.

Beyond this fundamental contract with the customer, there are many issues that customers prefer to have resolved quickly. These include simple requests for information, complaints, and major claims on the product or service the customer acquired.

The next two decision areas shift the focus to the benefits of retaining key customers. You start by benchmarking your company against industry standards. *What criteria are you measured against, and how good is your performance compared with the competition?* The last decision area brings everything together into a relative cost/benefit analysis of each customer relationship. *Are you reaping the rewards of Customer Service, what are they, and how much has it cost?*

On-Time Delivery

One of the biggest obligations a seller has to a buyer is to deliver on time what was purchased. Customers negotiate a due date and expect that it will be met, without exception. This is why delivery is a key performance criterion. Reducing time-related bottlenecks is critical in a just-in-time economy. Monitoring on-time delivery and order fill rate percentages can flag negative trends and enable faster customer service responses. It also provides Sales with information to solve potential issues before going on customer calls. Unfulfilled delivery expectations can also be important information for Accounts Receivable when checking on late payments from customers. This decision area can also uncover root causes of supply chain problems.

Tracking delivery timeliness by product, plant, and carrier will highlight potential deficiencies in key hand-off steps in the supply chain process. With better information, you can categorize different levels of timeliness and compare them to different customer delivery thresholds for a more detailed view of risk and recommended action.

GOALS	METRICS	DIMENSIONS
Average Lead-Time Days (#)	Avg. Quoted Lead Days (#)	Billing Customer
Order Fill Rate (%)	Avg. Sales per Order ($)	Industry Group
On-Time Unit Delivery (%)	Avg. Shipment Miles (#)	Industry
	Sales Order Count (#)	Category
	Shipments On-Time (#)	Customer Name
	Units Delivered On-Time (#)	Carrier/Distributor
	Units Shipped (#)	Distributor/Carrier Type
		Carrier
		Cust. Delivery On-Target Range
		Range
		Fiscal Week
		Fiscal Year
		Quarter
		Month
		Week
		Lead-Time Range
		Range
		On-Time Shipment Range
		Range
		Plants
		Plant
		Product SKU
		Product Line
		Brand
		SKU
		Shipment Type/Bill of Lading (#)
		Shipment Type
		Shipment Bill of Lading (#)
		Ship-To Location
		Region
		State/Province
		County
		City
		Zip Code/Postal Code

FUNCTION	DECISION ROLES	PRIMARY WORK	CONTRIBUTORY	STATUS
Customer Service				
	Executives	•		
	Managers	•		
	Analysts	•		
	Professionals	•		
Distribution				
	Executives	•		
	Managers	•		
	Analysts	•		
	Professionals	•		
Operations / Production				
	Executives			•
	Analysts		•	
Sales				
	Executives			•
	Managers		•	
	Analysts		•	
	Professionals		•	

In logistics, delivery times play an important role. For example, it is possible to determine, at any time, what percentage of orders a customer has received in the period X. It is also possible to identify which products are affected by a delayed delivery and also the reason for the delay. This is an important piece of information for customer support purposes, and it also helps trace the causes of processing problems or difficulties in the procurement chain. Another benefit is the detailed monitoring and control of warehousing, which is even more important when dealing with foodstuffs.

Andreas Speck, Head of Information Management, Kotányi GmbH

Information, Complaints, and Claims

Every complaint is also a proactive customer statement that you are not meeting expectations. It is an opportunity to listen to your customer, whether to a simple request for information, a complaint about product quality, or even a financial claim on returned goods. Experience shows that each call can be the tip of an iceberg—the one frustrated customer who calls may represent many more who don't bother. By tracking and categorizing these calls, you can gauge the severity of various risks and prevent them in the future.

There are three dimensions to monitoring the customer voice: frequency, coverage across customer segments, and type of issue. Simply counting complaints will not adequately reflect the nature or risk of a problem. For example, you may receive many complaints about paperwork and order identification errors, but these represent lower risk than a few product quality complaints that may lead to production delays for one or two large customers. In this example, a count of complaint frequency will not adequately reflect the risk of losing critical customers.

Claims are complaints that have been monetized. Perhaps goods have been damaged and the customer now needs compensation or replacement. Claims are a direct cost to the business, have a direct impact on customer profitability and, if poorly handled, lessen customer loyalty.

We have even made it possible to distribute calls in the Customer Contact Center using Skill Based Routing. In particular, this routes specific types of inquiries to those of our employees best able to deal with them effectively and efficiently.

Ton van den Dungen, Manager, Business Intelligence and Control, ENECO Energie

INFORMATION, COMPLAINTS, AND CLAIMS

GOALS	METRICS	DIMENSIONS	
Complaint Count (#)	Canceled Order Count (#)	Billing Customer	Complaint Status
Failed Orders (#)	Claim Payments ($)	Industry Group	Complaint Received
Returned Units (#)	Claim Payments (#)	Industry	Customer Location
	Claim Settlement ($)	Category	Region
	Claims (#)	Customer Name	State/Province
	Claims ($)	Carrier/Distributor	County
	Customer Recommendations (#)	Distributor/Carrier	Zip Code/Postal Code
	Damaged Units (#)	Type	End-Customer by Type
	Failed Orders ($)	Carrier	Type
	Returned Product ($/%)	Claim Status	Group
	Service Call Count (#)	Claims Received	Customer ID
		Claim Type	Fiscal Month
		Type	Year
		Identification (#)	Quarter
		Complaint	Month
		Type	
		Identification (#)	

FUNCTION	DECISION ROLES	PRIMARY WORK	CONTRIBUTORY	STATUS
Customer Service				
	Executives	•		
	Managers	•		
	Analysts	•		
	Professionals	•		
Distribution				
	Executives			•
	Managers		•	
	Analysts		•	
	Professionals		•	
Operations / Production				
	Executives			•
	Managers		•	
	Analysts		•	
	Professionals		•	
Sales				
	Executives			•
	Managers		•	
	Analysts		•	
	Professionals		•	
Finance				
	Executives	•		
	Analysts	•		

Service Benchmarks

Service benchmarks help evaluate how your customer service stacks up against industry standards. They measure response times and gaps affecting customer satisfaction.

Understanding the link between service benchmarks and customer sales/profitability is a key goal. For example, we may find that many small orders lead to complaints about incorrect order fulfillments and product returns. The high proportional cost of delivery for small orders, combined with the order errors, should make us question our value proposition. Perhaps by increasing the minimum order value we would solve two problems. First, there would be a reduction in per dollar workload, an improvement in order performance, and a reduction in returns. Second, the customer's perception of value may improve since delivery costs would be proportionally lower.

Internal metrics may include number of orders, sales order amount, number of service calls, and units shipped. External performance metrics may include delivery performance, problem resolution, customer satisfaction, response time, claims, and returns. Using standard industry criteria allows managers to compare external information from third-party assessments with internally driven customer surveys. Gaps in external information can uncover risks not picked up by internal monitoring. Such information can also identify the need for better external communications.

Combined with skilled analysis, service benchmarks can be used to adjust the business and customer proposition. You can summarize customer benchmarks by region and customer segment, and thereby offer a high-level overview or drill down into Customer Service performance.

Our customers are increasingly requiring immediate, direct access to their health transaction data in order to reduce healthcare costs while maintaining a high level of quality of care for their members. They also want to compare their actual experience to benchmark data that will add meaning and relevance to their own scores. Our ability to deliver that type of solution through a variety of Web-based reports and cubes has become a key differentiator between us and our competition. This capability is now a major tool in acquiring new business and retaining existing accounts and has also allowed us to reach our information management goal of becoming the pre-eminent healthcare information broker in the State of Tennessee.

Frank Brooks, Blue Cross Blue Shield, Tennessee

SERVICE BENCHMARKS

GOALS	METRICS	DIMENSIONS
Average Resolution Response Time (#)	Damaged Units (#)	Billing Customer
Customer Satisfaction Scorecard	Failed Orders (#)	Industry Group
Service Effectiveness Index	Lost Customer Count (#)	Industry
	Outstanding Service Issues (#)	Category
	Returned Product ($/%)	Customer Name
	Service Call Count (#)	Customer Location
		Region
		State/Province
		County
		Zip Code/Postal Code
		End-Customer Location
		Region
		State/Province
		County
		Zip Code/Postal Code
		Product Brand
		Product Line
		Brand
		Service Relationship Perspective
		Service Relationship Perspective

FUNCTION	DECISION ROLES	PRIMARY WORK	CONTRIBUTORY	STATUS
Customer Service				
	Executives	•		
	Managers	•		
	Analysts	•		
	Professionals	•		
Finance				
	Executives			•
Marketing				
	Executives			•
Product Development				
	Executives			•
Purchasing				
	Executives			•
Sales				
	Executives			•
	Analysts		•	

Service Value

This decision area combines costs and benefits to evaluate the value of the customer relationship. It segments customers by *who* they are and performance by how the company provides the service.

Quantifying customer risk issues and the efforts required to resolve them provides the cost overview. Some issues can be financially quantified, such as the number of calls received, cost per call, and dollar value of claims processed. Others, such as late deliveries or complaints, can be categorized through a service level index.

When determining cost, it is also important to understand how the relationship operates. *Does the customer communicate with you through efficient electronic means and direct access to internal support systems, or use less efficient means such as phone or fax?* Customer conversations that can be captured as data (i.e., electronic means) tend to indicate more efficient relationships. You can define sub-categories of complexity based on customer and transaction knowledge: for instance, by tagging relationships based on how many separate steps and hand-offs are required to complete the transaction.

At the same time, you need to categorize the benefits: for example, using a lifetime revenue metric or strategic value index based on expected revenue.

When Customer Service can analyze value and cost, it can avoid trading one for the other by setting more accurate priorities for use of resources. Poor service performance in simple channels implies that Customer Service should invest more in process automation and improved efficiency. Performance issues in complex channels point to increasing investment in skills, expertise, and decision-making support when analysis shows that the investment is worth it.

As an organization, we needed a solution that allowed us to report on KPIs in relation to key areas including customers. The index allows us to benchmark and report on performance in the customer service area.

Alex Mongard, MIS Analyst, Suncorp Metway

SERVICE VALUE

GOALS	METRICS	DIMENSIONS
Lifetime Profit ($)	Claims (#)	Aging Brackets
Service Cost (%)	Claims ($)	Range
Service Effectiveness Index	Complaint Count (#)	Billing Customer
	Customer Retention Cost ($)	Industry Group
	Customer Service Cost ($)	Industry
	Customer Visits (#)	Category
	Customers (#)	Customer Name
	Lost Customer Count (#)	Contracted Pay't Time
	Net Profit ($/%)	Range
	Outstanding Service Issues (#)	End-Customer by Type
	Receivables ($)	Type
		Group
		Customer ID
		Fiscal Month
		Year
		Quarter
		Month
		Product SKU
		Product Line
		Brand
		SKU

FUNCTION	DECISION ROLES	PRIMARY WORK	CONTRIBUTORY	STATUS
Customer Service				
	Executives	•		
	Managers	•		
	Analysts	•		
	Professionals	•		
Finance				
	Executives			•
	Managers		•	
	Analysts		•	
	Professionals		•	
Sales				
	Executives			•
	Managers		•	
	Analysts		•	
	Professionals		•	
Marketing				
	Executives			•
	Analysts		•	

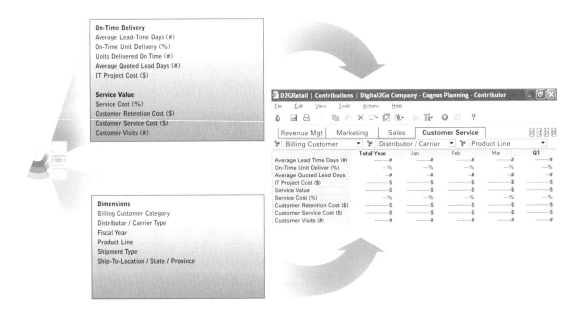

The On-Time Delivery and Service Value decision areas illustrate how the Customer Service function can monitor its performance, allocate resources, and set plans for future financial targets.

PRODUCT
DEVELOPMENT

Developing the Right Product, the Right Way, at the Right Time

Innovation is not the product of logical thought, although the result is tied to logical structure.
Albert Einstein

Product Development and its innovations are critical to your business and competitive ability. They represent the lifeblood of future business success. Moving into a new market area with a new product is a high-risk activity, and success is rare. Equally rare is successful development of a product that fundamentally changes the value proposition within an industry. Such new product investments require deep financial commitment.

Economic and industry cycles set the context for the importance of innovation, and therefore of Product Development. In fast-growing market sectors, product change is part of the competitive race, and significant investments are made in Product Development. In mature markets, where growth has slowed, investors rely on Product Development to assess the organization's future potential. New product developments can help slow the rate of market commoditization and protect margin erosion. In these mature market sectors, new developments are likely to be incremental, and small advantages can differentiate a leader from less successful followers.

Product Development delivers a pipeline of new products that determine the organization's future financial performance and signify confidence in the future of the business. Three significant barriers prevent it from delivering the required product changes in the most effective way.

Barrier 1: *Lack of information to determine strategy requirements*

Product Development embraces risk. The odds are stacked against continual success, especially if the business expects a BIG new product idea. Companies typically define Product Development success by sales or profit growth and the ROI expected within a given time period. Measuring financial performance is vital, but interpreting success too rigidly may lead the company to miss innovation opportunities. It is better to define and measure drivers and development milestones that affect the pipeline of new products. Similar to a portfolio investment strategy, these metrics allow for more opportunities (and therefore more failures) but let you know when to "fail fast" to satisfy the overarching profit or growth goal. Only a few product initiatives make it through to the final development stage. You can tolerate a calculated and controlled percentage of failure if the overall portfolio of new product developments is financially successful.

You may employ other aspects of portfolio investment strategy to determine your investment risk profile. How much money should you invest in new product development for low, medium, and high-risk ideas? Only a small proportion of investment should be devoted to high-risk big new ideas. Most investment should be in safer, incremental product development ideas. These will better match the current product range, and serve the dual purpose of protecting the existing business while extending the product proposition beyond what is currently offered.

Determining the right mix requires that Product Development benefit from insights into markets and customers. This means knowing what product features and price points could shift purchasing behavior, and understanding the operational costs and production implications of these. Only by integrating all these business inputs and information sweet spots can you achieve a well-developed new product proposition.

Barrier 2: *Product Development lacks the integrated business process information needed to develop targeted, comprehensive product offerings*

Product Development decisions affect and rely on Marketing, Sales, Finance, Operations, and other business departments. Without appropriate visibility, departmental barriers may get in the way and stymie the Product Development process. By monitoring the appropriate performance drivers, combined with appropriate incentives, you can improve the Product Development process from idea generation to alignment on priorities to engaging Finance, so the value of new products is understood and forecast.

Barrier 3: *Inability to measure and analyze the drivers of Product Development success*

New product pipelines depend on timely action. Speed to market paired with insight from "fast failures" are more important than perfection and indecision. Risk is part of the development process. "Calculated" failures are not necessarily negative; they may actually assist the development process. Failures can become stepping stones toward success.

Product Development must understand what drives success and failure. When developments reach a milestone, the company should test the product proposition in the market. The feedback you require will determine the means you select: selective customer input, larger external research, or a limited territorial launch.

No amount of testing guarantees success. Making the "go or no go" decision requires information sweet spots to allow the business to decide whether it needs more resources to improve the new offering, or if the cost of delay—either in lost revenue or lost competitive advantage—means the product must launch now.

From a Gamble to Controlled Product and Portfolio Development

Product Development combines many cross-functional requirements, balances risk, learns from failures, then generates a pipeline of timely new products. Accurate information is a key enabler of this process.

The Product Development process combines three key decision areas with associated information sweet spots.

- **Product and portfolio innovation** ➔ Which gaps in the product portfolio are addressable with the available resources, and what are the associated risks?

- **Product development milestones** ➔ How do we manage priorities and timings, and monitor risks as they change during the development process?

- **Market and customer feedback** ➔ What external verification process will enhance and confirm new product development opportunities?

Product and Portfolio Innovation

The product and portfolio decision area takes potential opportunities identified by Marketing and examines the practicalities in more depth. This decision area answers questions about the costs and benefits of adding new product features to fill product portfolio gaps, and how achievable these additions are given available resources. It also determines how achievable these opportunities are for the business and the risk of failure.

Innovation runs the gamut from incremental improvements to significant product "revolutions". Incremental developments include packaging changes, minor functional improvements, quality changes, and brand extensions. These developments are usually intended to fill gaps in the product portfolio. For instance, by improving the design, adding product capability, making the product more convenient to use, and increasing the price, the business may extend its offering into a profitable new segment.

At the high-risk end of innovation, you must measure time to market, implementation difficulty, external market or technical shifts, future scenario values, and estimated ROI. These metrics also help you prioritize threats and opportunities. For example, classifying Product Development activities into life-cycle categories balances short-term and long-term priorities. Measuring the difficulty of implementation ensures you don't choose impractical blue sky projects at the expense of what's needed in the short term.

Future scenario valuations with estimates of the upper and lower limits of potential sales and profits set the size of a project. ROI looks at the whole picture by including upfront investment, operating costs, and sales.

GOALS	METRICS	DIMENSIONS
New Product Market Share (%)	New Product Achievability Score/Risk (#)	Fiscal Month
New Product Sales ($)		Year
Product Develop. Cost ($)	New Product Breakeven (Time/$)	Quarter
		Month
	New Product Sales Potential ($)	Potential Projects
	New Products Developed (#)	R&D Project Type
	New Products in Market ($/%)	Project
	Products Modified (#)	Product Line
	Project Duration – Plan (Business Days)	Product Line
		Project Start Date
	Project Resource Days – Plan	Year
	Project Cost – Plan $	Quarter
	Tested Products (#)	Month
		Project Start Date
		Project Management
		Project Team
		Project Manager
		Project Member
		Project Completion Date
		Year
		Quarter
		Month
		Project Finish Date

FUNCTION	DECISION ROLES	PRIMARY WORK	CONTRIBUTORY	STATUS
Product Development				
	Executives	•		
	Managers	•		
	Analysts	•		
	Professionals	•		
Finance				
	Executives			•
	Analysts		•	
Marketing				
	Executives			•
	Analysts		•	
Sales				
	Executives			•
	Analysts		•	
Customer Service				
	Executives			•
	Analysts		•	
Operations / Production				
	Executives			•
	Analysts		•	

As a decision area, portfolio and product innovation recommends which opportunities are right for the business by aligning with other departments, particularly Marketing.

Product Development Milestones

This decision area is used to manage the Product Development process. It establishes milestones, manages and adjusts priorities and timings, and monitors risks as they change. Many companies use Stage-Gate® or phase-gate processes involving five stages for Product Development. These are a preliminary assessment, definition (market), development (product/cost), validation, and commercialization. Typically, a very low percentage of preliminary ideas pass through the final gate. Less formal processes still require that you answer questions such as: *What new product development ideas do we have? What is the scale of the identified opportunity? Do we have the skills in-house? What are the risks? Is the opportunity aligned with our strategic priorities? What are the likely financial rewards?*

Measuring performance milestones is critical to this decision area. The number of preliminary initiatives, how many milestones are passed before rejection, and the number of products ready for commercialization tell you about projects and how they pass through the process. Logging and evaluating the reasons for success or failure through these milestones will help you improve your Product Development process.

Regular planning and gap analysis reviews anchor the development process with business priorities. Without this focus and monitoring, the process may be sidelined by day-to-day concerns. It is critically important to ensure the success of all phases, from development to launch and full commercialization. Information that focuses and fine-tunes each stage, and provides incentives, is imperative to ensuring successful product launches.

GOALS	METRICS	DIMENSIONS
Product Develop. Cost ($)	Initiatives Rejected (#)	Fiscal Month
Product Develop. Lead Time (#)	New Initiatives (#)	Year
Project Completion by	New Product Launch Failures (#)	Quarter
Milestone (#/%)	New Products Developed (#)	Month
	Products Modified (#)	Forecast Scenario
	Proj. Duration – Business Days (#)	(Plan/Actual/Forecast)
	Proj. Duration – Variance (%)	Scenario
	Rejection Causes (#)	Product Development Milestone
	Tested Products (#)	Product Line
		Product Line
		Project
		Project/Program Type
		Project
		Project Start Date
		Year
		Quarter
		Month
		Project Start Date
		Project Management
		Project Team
		Project Manager
		Project Member
		Project Completion Date
		Year
		Quarter
		Month
		Project Finish Date

FUNCTION	DECISION ROLES	PRIMARY WORK	CONTRIBUTORY	STATUS
Product Development				
	Executives	•		
	Managers	•		
	Analysts	•		
	Professionals	•		
Finance				
	Executives			•
	Analysts		•	
Marketing				
	Executives			•
	Analysts		•	
Sales				
	Executives			•
	Analysts		•	
Operations / Production				
	Executives			•
	Analysts		•	

Market and Customer Feedback

The market and customer feedback decision area combines an external reality check with internal understanding of development opportunities and requirements. It is an extension of a product and portfolio gap analysis, generating external insights to use in gap assessment. There are many examples of overly engineered products that fail because they do not balance costs and those features actually valued by customers.

Market feedback and external verification as part of the development process are essential for success. The insights these activities produce let the organization understand what investments are necessary for new product features and determine if the business can afford them. In some cases, it may make sense to pull out of an opportunity area rather than make investments with an insufficient chance of payback. An information framework that uses this data can support and confirm Product Development decisions. This decision area is also a tool for creating cross-functional alignment and internal commitment to new product commercialization.

GOALS	METRICS	DIMENSIONS
Suggestion Cost ($)	External Verification Score (#)	Fiscal Month
Suggestion Value-Added Score (#)	Implementation Difficulty Score (#)	Year
	Suggestions (#)	Quarter
		Month
		Marketing Segment
		Market Segment
		Micro-Segment
		Product SKU
		Product Line
		Brand
		SKU
		Suggestion Priority Index
		Suggestion Type

FUNCTION	DECISION ROLES	PRIMARY WORK	CONTRIBUTORY	STATUS
Product Development				
	Executives	•		
	Managers	•		
	Analysts	•		
	Professionals	•		
Customer Service				
	Executives			•
	Managers		•	
	Analysts		•	
Sales				
	Executives			•
	Analysts		•	
Marketing				
	Executives			•
	Analysts		•	

Our business is driven by customers and our ability to understand what factors influence them adds incredible value.

Chris Boebel, IT Director, Delta Sonic Car Wash

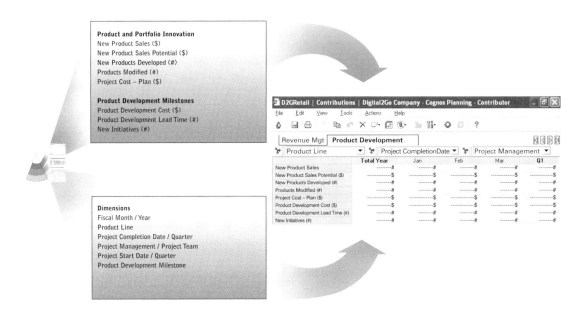

The Product and Portfolio Innovation and Product Development Milestones decision areas illustrate how the Product Development function can monitor its performance, allocate resources, and set plans for future financial targets.

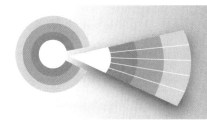

Winning at the Margin

A man who does not think and plan long ahead will find trouble right at his door.
Confucius

Operations is the delivery mechanism of the business: providing both what the business sells and how that product gets to market. It is an engine driving the work in purchasing, production, distribution, logistics, and inventory management. That engine depends on input from the frontline functions of the business—Sales, Marketing, and Finance.

Of all departments, Operations has dealt the longest with the competitive situation described in Tom Friedman's book *The World is Flat*. Offshore and outsourced production, technology-enabled process excellence, and supply chain integration are part of the relentless drive for lower costs. After more than a decade of investment and continuous improvement initiatives, companies have achieved what major cost savings are possible. Managing and winning at the margins is the new competitive area for Operations.

Three critical barriers prevent Operations from working these margins to deliver the best possible performance.

Barrier 1: *The operational back end can't see where it's going without the frontline's vision*

Operations depends on accurate and constantly updated information on what is required by customers. If you don't have accurate information about the demand (both volume and variety) for products in your pipeline, you stand to lose operational efficiency and profit margin. With better information and plans, you avoid emergency production runs to satisfy unforeseen customer demand. You reduce the need for production system change-over and setup, and so profit margins are higher. You can match production volume with customer demand to reduce inventory.

Barrier 2: *Process bottlenecks and downtime*

Operations continuously competes against time. Can this process be faster? Can workflow processes be re-engineered and simplified to gain time? The more steps between start and finish, the more bottlenecks and downtime risk may be hidden in them.

The time to complete a series of process tasks is inflated by waiting periods. In some situations, actual process time can be as low as five to ten percent of the total time from start to finished product. When only one-tenth of the time used is productive, reducing such waste is a worthy prize.

You must identify and eliminate predictable process time-wasters. While many solutions may be internal—such as innovation, changes in materials or equipment, or upgrades to IT infrastructure— you may decide your business is better served by outsourcing to a specialist with technical and scale advantages.

Information sweet spots help generate continuous intelligence loops on the real cost of bottlenecks and downtime, showing you the benefits of increased automation or specialization.

Barrier 3: *In a fast-paced, just-in-time economy, cost averages disguise cost reality*

With the just-in-time approach to Operations, new and changing customer requirements regularly affect workflow. It is no longer sufficient to use the standard costing analysis designed for long production runs. That approach may disguise significant variances in actual process performance costs. Customers who appear profitable on a standard cost basis may not be in fact.

By breaking down work processes into discrete activities and measuring them with accurate activity indicators, you can achieve real-time costing. The best indicators will vary with the situation. Some will be based on labor time used in machine setup. Others may directly measure the raw material used for a certain production run, or the number of quality tests required for a given customer product order. The more detailed this activity breakdown, the more accurate your understanding of actual costs. Understanding and analyzing the information sweet spots lets Operations identify process patterns and suggest cost savings.

For example, a business prints self-adhesive labels that range in complexity from two to five colors. A simple description of the work process steps includes:

- Specification
- Artwork
- Proofing
- Order confirmation
- Production planning
- Printer setup
- Production run
- Printer cleaning
- Maintenance
- Quality control
- Warehousing
- Dispatch
- Carrier routing

Analyzing the activity, the company realizes:

- More colors means higher costs
- Shorter runs mean 30 percent downtime
- The most demanding and "important" customer is rejecting and returning 10 percent of total deliveries while demanding smaller, more complex orders with just-in-time fulfillment

Based on this information, the business now understands that it is losing money on every order made by its "important" customer. Using a standard costing approach would never have highlighted this customer-specific cost reality.

Information sweet spots that let you understand what drives the larger cost categories will have an immediate and sizeable impact on managing actual costs.

Delivering on the Promise Made to the Customer

For Operations to win at the margins, every day and every shift must balance the need to reduce costs while staying agile enough to respond to new customer demands.

Operations has the responsibility to lead six core areas of the company's decision-making:

- **Purchasing and procurement** → Ensuring timely and cost-effective input of resources

- **Production and capacity** → Generating timely output in the face of uncertain demand, complicated processes, and variances in input

- **Inventory management** → Understanding the balance between holding cash and delivering on customer service requirements

- **Distribution and logistics** → Achieving efficient distribution and delivery

- **Cost and quality management** → Balancing the need to reduce costs with the equal requirement to deliver quality output

- **Process efficiency** → Designing a process to monitor and analyze performance benchmarks to find opportunities for greater efficiency

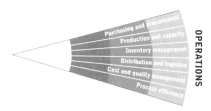

Purchasing and Procurement

The purchasing and procurement decision area manages both input costs and supply requirements. In many businesses, input costs account for up to 50 percent of total costs. Effectively managing them can bring savings directly to the bottom line. For every one percent gained in input cost savings, somewhere between 0.25 percent and 0.5 percent typically will be earned as profit. This is a significant return on investment when compared to other investments and project returns.

In addition to cost, the procurement personnel must ensure inputs arrive in a timely manner. Inputs arriving too late threaten production and customer delivery; inputs arriving too early cause unnecessary inventory buildup.

Managers must balance input costs with the production outputs required to satisfy customers. In the short term, your decisions must include how to respond to shortage problems, price increases, and delivery delays. For example, you must decide whether to tie up cash in five days of inventory to buffer against recent problems in delivery. Long-term decisions include determining your supplier strategy. For example, how do you balance the savings and/or better quality from exclusive supplier agreements against the risk of creating unacceptable dependencies?

These decisions require information on specifications, procurement tenders, price quotations, and vendor performance assessments. You cannot make the necessary purchasing trade-offs without access to information sweet spots. The better you understand the trade-offs, the more finely tuned is your ability to win at the margins.

GOALS	METRICS	DIMENSIONS
Purchase Price/Unit ($)	Actual Lead Days (#)	Fiscal Week
Reject Rate (%)	Contract Quantity (#)	Fiscal Year
Supplier Timeliness (%)	Contract Remaining (#)	Quarter
	Credit Rating (#)	Month
	List Price/Unit ($)	Week
	Purchase Order Cost ($)	Raw Material
	Purchase Orders (#)	Category
	Purchase Units (#)	Sub-Category
	Quality Rating (#)	RM Name
	Quoted Lead Days (#)	Tag #
	Supplier Discount ($)	RM Suppliers
	Supplier Discount (%)	Type
	Supplier Perf. Rating	Supplier
		Shipment Type/Bill of Lading (#)
		Shipment Type
		Shipment Bill of Lading (#)
		Vendor Status
		Status
		Contract/Spot

FUNCTION	DECISION ROLES	PRIMARY WORK	CONTRIBUTORY	STATUS
Purchasing				
	Executives	•		
	Managers	•		
	Analysts	•		
	Professionals	•		
Distribution				
	Executives			•
	Managers		•	
	Analysts		•	
	Professionals		•	
Operations / Production				
	Executives			•
	Managers		•	
	Analysts		•	
Audit				
	Executives			•
	Managers	•		
	Analysts	•		

Production and Capacity

Without product, there is no business. Accordingly, this decision area is the backbone of the business.

Production management depends on order fulfillment and expected sales information. Ideally, you know product demand well in advance to be able to plan capacity and schedule production runs for given products. This minimizes downtime and maximizes machine loadings. Changing a schedule, especially for an urgent customer need, means rearranging existing production schedules and results in extra setup time, change-over time, idle time, and lost capacity. *The bottom line?* It reduces your ability to win at the margins.

As with any chain of interconnected links, changes in demand affect your input requirements. The domino effect of changes spreads across the whole Operations process, creating a series of costly capacity management responses.

GOALS	METRICS	DIMENSIONS
Backlog (%)	Avg. Units per Order (#)	Fiscal Week
Capacity Utilization (%)	Avg. Units/Production Run (#)	Fiscal Year
Systems Up Time (%)	Fixed Production Cost ($/%)	Quarter
	Marginal Production Cost ($/%)	Month
	Production Hours (#)	Week
	Production/Batch Runs (#)	Machines
	Scheduled Production Hours (#)	Equipment Type
	Scrap Unit (#)	Machine
	Set-Up Time (#)	Mfg. Product Run Number
	Units in Production Schedule (#)	Product Line
	Units Produced (#)	SKU
	Units Produced/Hour (#)	Component
	Units Reworked (#)	Part Number
	Variable Production Cost ($/%)	Run Number
	WIP End (#)	Organization
	WIP In (#)	Division
	WIP Out (#)	Department
		Org. Code
		Production Process
		Production Process
		Work Function

FUNCTION	DECISION ROLES	PRIMARY WORK	CONTRIBUTORY	STATUS
Operations / Production				
	Executives	•		
	Managers	•		
	Analysts	•		
	Professionals	•		
Purchasing External				
	Executives			•
	Managers		•	
	Analysts		•	
	Professionals		•	
Finance				
	Executives			•
	Analysts		•	
Sales				
	Executives			•
	Analysts		•	
Customer Service				
	Executives			•
	Analysts		•	

To counter this, you must communicate new information immediately so that Operations can adjust its schedule in the most effective manner. You must also communicate potential delays to Customer Service for resolution. Closely monitoring this ebb and flow of changing circumstances through production information sweet spots lets Operations maximize its use of production capacity.

Inventory Management

Shipping appropriately bundled products to fill customer orders is the concern of the inventory management decision area. Balancing customer requirements, speed of order fulfillment, and the volume of buffer stock you need to hold are key.

The principle of holding buffer inventory is simple—but the larger your product range, the greater the complications. If a business has 5,000 specific product items and 10,000 customers, there are 50 million possible product/customer combinations to monitor and serve effectively. [*Note:* with bundling combinations, many more than 50 million.] The fact that buffer stock ties up cash compounds the urgency of decisions. If you hold one month of buffer inventory, one month of production has not earned a return—equivalent to more than eight percent (one-twelfth) of a year's production cost.

But inventory management must also determine the financial and customer consequences of removing buffer stock from inventory. Tying up 40 to 50 percent of your inventory with products that are rarely ordered makes no sense unless key customers highly value these products.

Understanding the full implications of these decisions requires access to information sweet spots. In the

GOALS	METRICS	DIMENSIONS
Inventory ($)	Avg. FG (#)	Fiscal Week
Inventory / Days (%)	Avg. FG ($)	Fiscal Year
Inventory Turns (#)	Avg. Units per Order (#)	Quarter
Product SKUs (#)	FG End (#)	Month
	FG End ($)	Week
	FG In (#)	Product SKU
	FG Inv. Carrying Cost ($)	Product Line
	FG Out (#)	Brand
	Product SKU Order Frequency (#)	SKU
	Time since Last Order (#)	Warehouse
		Region
		District
		Warehouse

FUNCTION	DECISION ROLES	PRIMARY WORK	CONTRIBUTORY	STATUS
Operations / Production				
	Executives	•		
	Managers	•		
	Analysts	•		
	Professionals	•		
Distribution				
	Executives			•
	Managers		•	
	Analysts		•	
	Professionals		•	
Finance				
	Executives			•
	Managers		•	
	Analysts		•	
	Professionals		•	
Purchasing				
	Executives			•
	Managers		•	
	Analysts		•	
	Professionals		•	
Audit				
	Executives			•
	Managers	•		
	Professionals	•		
Customer Service				
	Executives			•
	Analysts		•	

example above, it means knowing the total annual sales and profit value of each of the 5,000 product items. Most will earn less than one percent of total margin. *Which ones? Of these, how many go to your most important customers, and are they seen as critical components of the order?* If order frequency is low and irregular, the case for culling these product items increases. Even if significant savings will result from this product cull, you must align the decision with input from other functions such as Sales and Customer Service. *How should you handle the notification, and what are the contingency measures if key customers complain?* Sales does not like bringing bad news to customers and expects a clear justification for such business decisions. Factual reasons will be useful when communicating your rationale to customers.

Distribution and Logistics

This decision area includes managing quality, cost, and timeliness of distribution and delivery. Short-term issues require the handling of customer orders and shipping using the most efficient routing, scheduling, and equipment. Long-term issues require determining whether you can reduce mileage costs, improve delivery execution, and ideally exceed customer service needs.

The operational infrastructure to distribute and deliver customer goods is intricate and costly. Many companies work with third-party carriers, distributors, or wholesalers for their expertise. Distributors specialize in particular channels, routes, and/or territories, and can distribute more quickly and efficiently than most manufacturers. Strategically placed distribution warehouses can be an advantage to, and extension of, your sales force.

While outsourcing makes sense on many levels, it does mean you lose direct control and have to accept the risks that come with loss of control. Managing such risks requires negotiating and monitoring distributor agreements with clear terms and commercial guidelines.

GOALS	METRICS	DIMENSIONS	
Damaged Units (%)	Avg. Actual Lead Days (#)	Billing Customer	Product SKU
Distribution Cost ($)	Avg. Quoted Lead Days (#)	Industry Group	Product Line
On-Time Unit Delivery (%)	Damaged Units ($)	Industry	Brand
Price/lb/100miles ($)	Delivery Frequency (#)	Category	SKU
	Insurance Cost ($)	Customer Name	Shipment Type/BOL #
	Lead Days (%)	Carrier/Distributor	Shipment Type
	Order Size (#)	Distributor/Carrier Type	Shipment BOL #
	Shipments On Time (#)	Carrier	Ship-To Location
	Total Shipments (#)	Carrier Activity Status	Region
	Units Delivered On Time (#)	Activity Status	State/Province
	Units Shipped (#)	Carrier	County
		Carrier Region	City
		Region	Zip Code/Postal Code
		State/Province	
		County	
		Zip Code/Postal Code	
		Fiscal Month	
		Year	
		Quarter	
		Month	

FUNCTION	DECISION ROLES	PRIMARY WORK	CONTRIBUTORY	STATUS
Distribution				
	Executives	•		
	Managers	•		
	Analysts	•		
	Professionals	•		
Customer Service				
	Executives			•
	Managers		•	
	Analysts		•	
	Professionals		•	
Finance				
	Executives			•
	Managers		•	
	Analysts		•	
	Professionals		•	
Purchasing				
	Executives			•
	Managers		•	
	Analysts		•	
	Professionals		•	
Sales				
	Executives			•
	Analysts		•	
Operations / Production				
	Analysts		•	

Identifying, managing, and evaluating the most effective distribution and logistics routes for customers or prospects draws on the following information sweet spots:

- **Order processing** ➔ editing, recording, credit control, stock allocation, vehicle route, delivery sequence, customer delivery requests
- **Handling characteristics** ➔ ease of handling, and stacking, susceptibility to damage, special requirements (e.g., temperature)
- **Packaging** ➔ duration and type of journey, security, insurance
- **Routing and scheduling** ➔ order size, transport capacity, customer destination network, delivery frequency

Cost and Quality Management

In cost and quality management, you balance cost savings in one area against potential rework, rejects, downtime, or customer complaints. Purchasing may find a new, lower-cost supplier but the consequence may be higher scrap rates. *What is best for the business?*

You need to understand cost variances and their impacts. By contrasting cost differences, you can benchmark performance, identify patterns, and understand the root causes of cost differences. You also need to understand and analyze the value and cost of preventative measures that ensure quality such as training, appraising incoming materials, manufacturing processes, and inspections. The more you examine measurable work activities and the more detailed your breakdown of costs, the more detailed your understanding will be of the root causes of variances in those costs. Measuring and monitoring must be integrated with quality expectations to understand the effect of changes.

GOALS	METRICS	DIMENSIONS
Failure Cost ($)	Defects (#)	Fiscal Month
QC Reject Rate (%)	QC Cost ($)	Year
	QC Defects Fixed (#)	Quarter
	QC Units Sampled (#)	Month
	Scrap Cost ($)	Mfg. Product Component
	Scrap Unit (#)	Product Line
		SKU
		Component
		Product SKU
		Product Line
		Brand
		SKU
		QC Defect Issues
		QC Defect Issues
		QC Tolerance Standards
		QC Tolerance Ranges

FUNCTION	DECISION ROLES	PRIMARY WORK	CONTRIBUTORY	STATUS
Operations / Production				
	Executives	•		
	Managers	•		
	Analysts	•		
	Professionals	•		
Product Development				
	Executives			•
	Managers		•	
	Analysts		•	
	Professionals		•	
Audit				
	Executives			•
	Managers		•	
	Professionals		•	
Customer Service				
	Executives			•
	Analysts		•	
Finance				
	Executives			•
	Analysts		•	
Marketing				
	Executives			•
	Analysts		•	
Purchasing				
	Executives			•
	Analysts		•	
Sales				
	Executives			•
	Analysts		•	
Distribution				
	Analysts		•	

Process Efficiency

Process efficiency management looks at ways to improve operation and supply chains. This means looking for performance outliers and understanding why they occur. There are three areas where well-designed comparative performance metrics can make the difference between an industry follower and a leader:

- Internal operational processes
- External developments and trends
- Competitive benchmarking

Your internal operational processes are most familiar to you, and the easiest to analyze. For example, if Purchasing's "cost per dollar of purchase" is a benchmark, then an unusual increase in this index may indicate two things. Either purchasing costs have increased or purchases have decreased. You must determine whether purchasing efficiency has gone down or if sales have slumped. Another possible benchmark is "dollars of sales per order". If this metric is decreasing, it can indicate that the business is filling more orders for the same dollar total in sales. This may mean that costs have risen without an accompanying increase in sales—but it may instead indicate that you need to re-engineer the business to handle smaller orders.

Taking advantage of external developments and trends requires looking outside your company. *Should you shift to low labor cost economies for cheaper manufacturing or services such as call centers? Are there new manufacturing techniques, equipment, or technologies that can introduce dramatic efficiencies?* Failing to follow up on these external efficiency developments may jeopardize your competitive position.

Beyond this focus, many leading businesses extend their monitoring activities to their competitors. Simple comparative benchmarks such as sales per employee, volume output per employee, inventory levels, number of warehouses, and others will help identify performance differences. With these identified, you can determine the actions you need to take.

GOALS	METRICS	DIMENSIONS
Operational Failures (#)	Avg. Units/Production Run (#)	Fiscal Month
Process Cost ($)	Downtime Cost ($)	Year
Process Value-Add ($)	Maintenance Cost ($)	Quarter
		Month
	Process Steps (#)	Mfg. Product Component
	Production/Batch Runs (#)	Product Line
	Scheduled Production Hours (#)	SKU
	Set-Up Cost ($)	Component
		Product SKU
		Product Line
		Brand
		SKU
		Production Process
		Production Process
		Work Function

FUNCTION	DECISION ROLES	PRIMARY WORK	CONTRIBUTORY	STATUS
Production				
	Executives	•		
	Analysts	•		
	Managers	•		
	Professionals	•		
Finance				
	Executives			•
	Analysts		•	
IT / Systems				
	Executives			•
	Analysts		•	
Purchasing				
	Executives			•
	Analysts		•	
Sales				
	Analysts		•	
Distribution				
	Analysts		•	

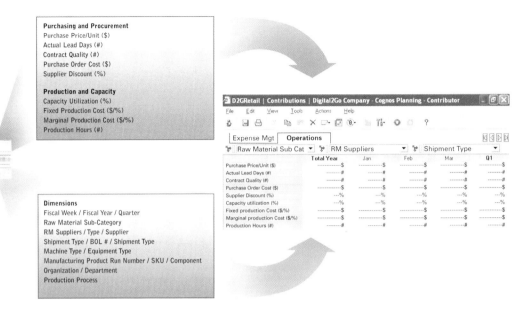

Purchasing and Procurement
Purchase Price/Unit ($)
Actual Lead Days (#)
Contract Quality (#)
Purchase Order Cost ($)
Supplier Discount (%)

Production and Capacity
Capacity Utilization (%)
Fixed Production Cost ($/%)
Marginal Production Cost ($/%)
Production Hours (#)

Dimensions
Fiscal Week / Fiscal Year / Quarter
Raw Material Sub-Category
RM Suppliers / Type / Supplier
Shipment Type / BOL # / Shipment Type
Machine Type / Equipment Type
Manufacturing Product Run Number / SKU / Component
Organization / Department
Production Process

The Purchasing and Procurement and Production and Capacity decision areas illustrate how the Operations function can monitor its performance, allocate resources, and set plans for future financial targets.

Management or Administration of Human Capital?

Did you realize that approximately 42% of the average company's intellectual capital exists only within its employees' heads?

Thomas Brailsford

Your people interact with your customers to generate revenue. They introduce the small and significant innovations that move your company forward. They set the strategic direction for your organization and then put those strategies into operation. Human capital is your most valuable asset.

It is also typically *undervalued*.

Helping the organization recognize human capital as a valuable asset and competitive differentiator is the strategic role of Human Resources.

Human Resources must demonstrate positive ROI from human capital investments. Human Resources guides the alignment of employee roles, job functions, talent, and individual performance with business results and goals. It finds, engages, assesses, develops, and retains the talent that drives the business. It manages administrative requirements such as payroll, benefits, the recruitment process, policy standards, and holiday and sick leave tracking. Human Resources also acts on behalf of employees, and in this respect is the *conscience* of the organization.

Three critical barriers prevent Human Resources fulfilling its strategic role and hamper it tactically.

Barrier 1: *Lack of information in defining and selling the role and business value of Human Resources*

Senior management expects every business unit to generate reports and analysis that measure performance against plan. Human Resources is no different. Research suggests that better human capital practices lead to higher financial returns and have a direct impact on share price. Investors, for example, scrutinize headcount and salary or wage ratios. Historically, however, Human Resources has focused more on managing administrative requirements than on communicating—and selling—the business value of human capital management.

While managing administrative requirements is essential, there are other critical strategic aspects of managing human capital. Fulfilling them requires that Human Resources understands the strategic objectives of the business, translates these into job skill requirements and individual capabilities, and designs an appropriate performance tracking process. Human Resources should first assign a value to each human capital asset and, by communicating this value, underline the importance of managing its performance.

> Base salary expenses +
> Recruiting expenses +
> Transfer expenses +
> Training expenses +
> Bonus and/or incentive expenses +
> Stock option grant value (estimate) =
> _____
> **Human capital asset investment**

Tracking these factors allows Human Resources to better manage human capital assets by asking the following questions. *What is the quality and value of the employee/employer relationship? What are the training and development needs in this specific case? How should we provide incentives and motivation for employees?* Answers may come from reports on staff turnover, high-performer retention rates, headcount growth, role definitions, job productivity, and individual performance monitoring.

Assessing comparative productivity ratios such as revenue to headcount also helps manage resource requirements, both short term and long term. These information sweet spots demonstrate the asset's strategic business value to the organization. Lack of such information impairs Human Resources's ability to fulfill its strategic role.

Barrier 2: *Lack of visible and consistent Human Resources practices*

The credibility and business value of Human Resources is often compromised by a lack of consistency in decisions and by insufficient information. This allows an "informal network" to bias the selection and promotion of employees. As a strategic partner in the business, Human Resources should understand and define the factors defining success for employees. *Does the business depend on customer service? On innovation? Low cost?* Based on this understanding, Human Resources can institute practices that guide employees toward consistent and measurable milestones, creating a structured process.

Implementing visible and consistent practices requires quality information. You will not achieve the consistency you need if policy documents, performance reviews, career objectives, and compensation assessments are not combined and positioned within a larger structure. Consistency requires a well-defined and structured process shared across the organization.

You also need a clearly defined process for collecting Human Resources information. *How should this data be stored and retrieved? Can this mostly qualitative information be analyzed usefully, and synthesized into a metric framework?* With such a synthesis, Human Resources gains the ability to compare and contrast different performance drivers. Identifying, managing, and retaining talented individuals is a key competitive requirement, and consistent information and management practices allow you to achieve this.

Barrier 3: *Human Resources has a natural ally in IT but is not fully leveraging this asset*

Both Human Resources and IT strive to position themselves within an organization as driving business value instead of expense. They can be seen as two sides of the same coin.

Human Resources is responsible for job design and ensuring that the right skills and competencies are developed or acquired to fill these jobs. In turn, performance in these jobs is defined and measured against goals and objectives. In this sense, Human Resources's information needs to mirror the performance to be monitored, analyzed, and planned for in a given job. IT must understand a user's responsibilities in order to include that user in planning where functionality is deployed. Both Human Resources and IT must understand how software tools and skills drive greater productivity. As performance management information becomes more consistent and reliable, it will also enhance the performance and compensation process for which Human Resources is responsible.

Earning a Place at the Executive Table

Human Resources decision areas:

- **Organization and staffing** ➔ What job functions, positions, roles, and capabilities are required to drive the business forward?

- **Compensation** ➔ How should we reward our employees to retain and motivate them for full performance?

- **Talent and succession** ➔ What are the talent and succession gaps we must address to ensure sustained performance?

- **Training and development** ➔ What training and development do we need to maximize employee performance; is there a clear payback?

- **Benefits** ➔ How do we manage costs and incentives?

Organization and Staffing

In a human capital discussion, first define the organization's requirements. *What are the job functions, positions, roles, and capabilities required to drive the business forward?* The organization chart becomes a road map highlighting staffing needs and the necessary hierarchy. From this road map, Human Resources further refines the role, position, and skill requirements needed to accurately evaluate candidates and current employees.

Organization and staffing analysis is a core Human Resources role. Typically, companies align staffing reports with information about position planning, staffing mix, and staffing transaction activities (new hires, transfers, retirements, terminations, etc.). Analyzing this data helps the company monitor policy standards and legal requirements. Human Resources must track issues such as employee overtime, absenteeism, pay/tax, and termination/retirement to ensure they are managed correctly.

In addition, when senior management discusses strategy and corporate goals, there are typically accompanying reports that show headcount by division/department, turnover rates, loss trends, and high-level project status. These reports help ensure resources are aligned with the global priorities of the company.

GOALS	METRICS	DIMENSIONS	
Avg. Tenure (#)	Absenteeism Days (#)	Employee Decision Role	Job Types
Employee Turnover (%)	Applications per Vacancy (#)	Work Function	Job Type
Headcount (#)	Avg. Age (#)	Decision Role	Job
	New Hires (#)	Employees	Organization
	Open Position Count (#)	Full-Time/Part-Time	Division
	Rejected Job Offers (#)	Employee Name	Department
	Retirements (#)	Fiscal Month	Org. Code
	Sick Leave Days (#)	Year	Plan/Actual Scenario
	Terminations (#)	Quarter	Scenario
	Transfers (#)	Month	
	Work Function Count (#)	Job Grade Level	
	Work Time Actual Hrs. (#)	Job Level	
		Job Name	

FUNCTION	DECISION ROLES	PRIMARY WORK	CONTRIBUTORY	STATUS
Human Resources				
	Executives	•		
	Managers	•		
	Analysts	•		
	Professionals	•		
Audit				
	Executives			•
	Managers		•	
	Professionals		•	
IT / Systems				
	Executives		•	
	Professionals		•	
Customer Service				
	Executives		•	
Distribution				
	Executives		•	
Finance				
	Executives		•	
Marketing				
	Executives		•	
Operations / Production				
	Executives		•	
Purchasing				
	Executives		•	
Product Development				
	Executives		•	
Regulatory				
	Executives		•	
Sales				
	Executives		•	

Compensation

Compensation review examines salary costs—existing and planned—across the workforce, as well as how these costs are reflected at the departmental, business unit, and global levels. This decision area defines how you need to reward your employees to retain them and motivate them for the best possible performance. Profiles on base pay, merit increases, promotions, and incentives help you decide the total compensation strategy and individual employee compensation. With this complexity comes the need for systematic methods for identifying and analyzing pay increases, bonuses, and incentive awards. Many organizations now require that performance reviews are ongoing; tracking the review process is therefore a requirement. Plans and reports on the coverage, completeness, and timeliness of the review process confirm your progress against rewards management, career planning, and development targets.

GOALS	METRICS	DIMENSIONS	
Avg. Compensation Increase ($)	Avg. Compensation Increase ($)	Compensation Program	Job Grade Level
Avg. Compensation Increase (%)	Bonus/Incentive Costs ($)	Program Type	Job Level
Compensation Cost ($)	Compensation Increases (#)	Program	Job Name
	Compensation Review (#)	Diversity	Job Types
	Employee Promotions (#)	Diversity Class	Job Type
	Employees (#)	Employee	Job
	Salary ($)	Employees	O/T Eligibility Status
	Skills Rating Gap (%)	Full-Time/Part-Time	Exempt/Non-Exempt
	Skills Rating Index (#)	Employee Name	Organization
		Fiscal Month	Division
		Year	Department
		Quarter	Org. Code
		Month	Work Function
			Work Function

FUNCTION	DECISION ROLES	PRIMARY WORK	CONTRIBUTORY	STATUS
Human Resources				
	Executives	•		
	Managers	•		
	Analysts	•		
	Professionals	•		
Finance				
	Executives		•	
	Managers		•	
	Analysts	•		
	Professionals		•	
Audit				
	Executives			•
	Managers	•		
	Professionals	•		
Sales				
	Executives		•	
	Analysts		•	
Customer Service				
	Executives		•	
Distribution				
	Executives		•	
IT / Systems				
	Executives		•	
Operations / Production				
	Executives		•	
Marketing				
	Executives		•	
Purchasing				
	Executives		•	
Product Development				
	Executives		•	

Talent and Succession

A company talent and succession review lets management see how current and planned business skills and technical qualifications meet today's and tomorrow's requirements. Human Resources must understand both the skill gaps and talent risks within the organization and plan accordingly. Talent review lets Human Resources assess recruiting, staff transfer, and succession planning needs. Other data such as turnover analysis, average tenure, and time in position also help define succession plans.

GOALS	METRICS	DIMENSIONS	
Employee Satisfaction Index (#)	Avg. Performance Rating	Core Competency	Job Types
	Avg. Skill/Experience Rating (Current)	Skill Type	Job Type
Succession Gaps (#)		Skill	Job
Talent Gaps (#)	Avg. Skill/Experience Rating (Target)	Employees	Organization
		Full-Time/Part-Time	Division
	Avg. Tenure (years)	Employee Name	Department
	Retirements (#)	Fiscal Month	Org. Code
	Skills Rating Gap (%)	Year	Work Function
		Quarter	Work Function
	Skills Rating Index (#)	Month	
	Succession Reviews (#)	Job Grade Level	
		Job Level	
		Job Name	

FUNCTION	DECISION ROLES	PRIMARY WORK	CONTRIBUTORY	STATUS
Human Resources				
	Executives	•		
	Managers	•		
	Analysts	•		
	Professionals	•		
Customer Service				
	Executives			•
	Managers		•	
Distribution				
	Executives			•
	Managers		•	
Finance				
	Executives			•
	Managers		•	
IT / Systems				
	Executives			•
	Managers		•	
Marketing				
	Executives			•
	Managers		•	
Operations / Production				
	Executives			•
	Managers		•	
Purchasing				
	Executives			•
	Managers		•	
Product Development				
	Executives			•
	Managers		•	
Sales				
	Executives			•
	Managers		•	

Training and Development

When you've defined the organization's required skill sets (to match employee abilities with position descriptions), the next logical decision area is determining the training and development needs of those employees. This decision area lets you review employee competencies and understand the value of improving them. *How much development time and training cost is being invested, and is there visible evidence of the benefit?* With training and development analysis, Human Resources gains a systematic picture of all training investment.

GOALS	METRICS	DIMENSIONS	
Skills Rating Gap (%)	Employees (#)	Employee Decision Role	Job Types
Training and Development Cost ($)	Skills Rating Index (#)	Work Function	Job Type
	Training and Development Cost Change (%)	Decision Role	Job
Training & Devlopment Cost/Payroll (%)	Training Days (#)	Employees	Organization
	Training Events Completed (#)	Full-Time/Part-Time	Division
	Training Events Planned (#)	Employee Name	Department
		Fiscal Month	Org. Code
		Year	Plan/Actual Scenario
		Quarter	Scenario
		Month	Training Course
		Job Grade Level	Type
		Job Level	Course
		Job Name	Work Function
			Work Function

FUNCTION	DECISION ROLES	PRIMARY WORK	CONTRIBUTORY	STATUS
Human Resources				
	Executives	•		
	Managers	•		
	Analysts	•		
	Professionals	•		
Customer Service				
	Executives			•
	Managers		•	
Distribution				
	Executives			•
	Managers		•	
Finance				
	Executives			•
	Managers		•	
IT / Systems				
	Executives			•
	Managers		•	
Marketing				
	Executives			•
	Managers		•	
Operations / Production				
	Executives			•
	Managers		•	
Purchasing				
	Executives			•
	Managers		•	
Product Development				
	Executives			•
	Managers		•	
Sales				
	Executives			•
	Managers		•	

Benefits

The benefits decision area lets you manage the costs of healthcare programs, savings and pension plans, stock purchase programs, and other similar initiatives. It compares the company's benefits with those of the competition. Benchmarking benefits helps determine whether you are aligned with the marketplace. As well, because investors scrutinize benefits costs for risk and liability, understanding this area helps demonstrate your company's management acumen.

GOALS	METRICS	DIMENSIONS
Benefit Cost Increase (%)	Avg. Benefits per Employee ($)	Benefits Program
Benefit Costs ($)	Benefit Market Comparison	Program Type
Benefit Costs/Payroll (%)	Index (#)	Program
	Benefits Approved (#)	Claim Type
	Benefits Claimed (#)	Type
	Benefits Claimed ($)	Identification #
	Benefits Paid ($)	Employees
	Payroll ($)	Full-Time/Part-Time
		Employee Name
		Fiscal Month
		Year
		Quarter
		Month
		Insurance Carrier
		Distributor/Carrier Type
		Carrier
		Insurance Coverage
		Type
		Coverage
		Job Grade Level
		Job Level
		Job Name
		Loss Control Program
		Program
		Organization
		Division
		Department
		Org. Code

FUNCTION	DECISION ROLES	PRIMARY WORK	CONTRIBUTORY	STATUS
Human Resources				
	Executives	•		
	Managers	•		
	Analysts	•		
	Professionals	•		
Audit				
	Executives			•
	Managers	•		
	Professionals	•		
Finance				
	Executives			•
	Managers		•	
	Analysts	•		

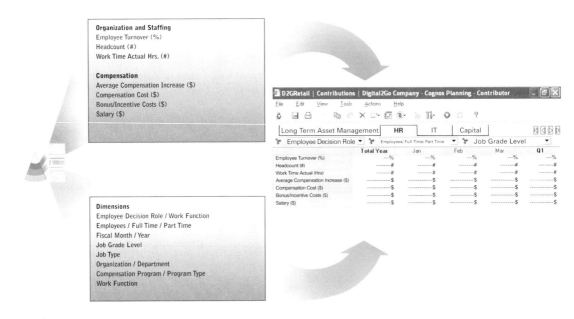

Organization and Staffing
Employee Turnover (%)
Headcount (#)
Work Time Actual Hrs. (#)

Compensation
Average Compensation Increase ($)
Compensation Cost ($)
Bonus/Incentive Costs ($)
Salary ($)

Dimensions
Employee Decision Role / Work Function
Employees / Full Time / Part Time
Fiscal Month / Year
Job Grade Level
Job Type
Organization / Department
Compensation Program / Program Type
Work Function

The Organization and Staffing and Compensation decision areas illustrate how the Human Resources function can monitor its performance, allocate resources, and set plans for future financial targets.

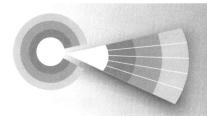

A Pathfinder to Better Performance

Our Age of Anxiety is, in great part, the result of trying to do today's jobs with yesterday's tools.
Marshall McLuhan

IT can be to the company what high-tech firms have been to the economy—a catalyst for change and an engine driving rapid growth. Of course, the opposite is also true: IT failures can seriously harm the company.

Why? Technology and information have become so important to how companies operate that even small changes can dramatically affect many areas of the business. This reality is reflected in the amount of IT assets accumulated over years due to large IT budgets, often second only to payroll in size. *How many of these assets are still underleveraged, for whatever reason? What impact on results would an across-the-board 10 percent increase in return on IT assets (ROA) have?*

Clearly, the stakes are high. And yet, IT is often seen as a simple support function or an expense ripe for outsourcing. It is rarely seen as an enabler or creative pathfinder for the business.

IT's daily pressures often derive from thankless, sometimes no-win tasks, such as ensuring core service levels of up-time, data quality, security, and compliance. Beyond these basic operations—"keeping the lights on"—IT must also respond to the never-ending and always-changing needs of their business customers. The challenge of managing their expectations is intensified by the pressure to reduce costs, do more with less, and even outsource major capabilities.

Companies often cite poor alignment of IT with other functions as the key challenge. IT, however, can be the pathfinder that helps the company discover a new way to drive value and maximize ROI and ROA. Unfortunately, the opportunity for IT to demonstrate this is often blocked by three common barriers.

Barrier 1: *Effective alignment cannot succeed without a common language and unifying map*

IT must be well aligned with the business. Much has been written about processes for achieving greater alignment in IT decisions. These include:

- Securing senior executive sponsorship

- Implementing gating procedures and ROI justifications for project approvals

- Establishing steering committees and business partnering roles and responsibilities

However, for any of these processes to be successful, IT and the company as a whole need to share a common language and unifying map.

This is really about building a relevant business context for what IT can do. The language and map must reflect a fundamental understanding of what issues matter to the success of the company. Then you can form a credible view on how IT capabilities can help. The map must show how IT capabilities fit among the company's other functions, processes, decisions and, most important, goals. It must show who benefits from these capabilities. And it must be able to communicate the strengths and weaknesses of these IT capabilities across a range of infrastructure, applications, and information, as well as how to manage them. Think of it as a Google™ Earth tool for IT. Zoom in on business objectives and evaluate different technical options based on an understanding of detailed capabilities.

Business Visibility

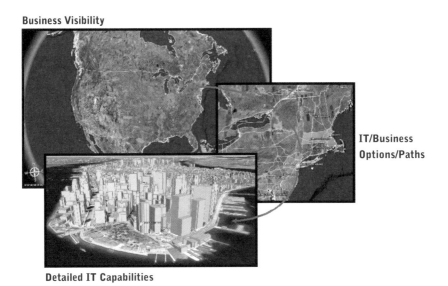

IT/Business Options/Paths

Detailed IT Capabilities

The common language and unifying map should include the fundamental anchors of metadata (such as customer, product, and location) and standard business rules. Finally, it must also clarify and explain IT terminology. Non-technical audiences should be able to understand the impact of IT in business terms and answer some fundamental questions, including:

- Where are we today, where do we want to be, and how can we get there?

- What business processes and strategic goals are being negatively affected?

- How could IT drive better business performance? Which users stand to benefit?

- How well do multiple, discrete IT assets combine to fulfill complex business performance requirements?

- What information do you need to drive better decision-making capabilities, in terms of content (measures and dimensions), business rules (metadata), and use (functionality)?

- What financial and human resources do you require to fulfill your goals?

- How should costs be aggregated and allocated to reflect actual use?

- What are the cost/benefit trade-offs between alternative technical options?

Barrier 2: *The difficulty of developing more credible, closed-loop measurements of IT's value to the company*

It is standard practice within most IT departments to evaluate the return on investment for projects and initiatives, and measure the cost/benefit of various IT capabilities. The challenge comes in developing a value measurement system that:

- Is credible with Finance and users alike

- Provides insight into cause and effect drivers

- Goes beyond point measurement to reflect the entire company

- Is consistent across projects, departments, and business units

- Provides a closed loop so that results can be compared to the plan and lessons learned

Fundamentally, IT creates value by improving operational efficiency and/or effectiveness, but defining what this actually means isn't straightforward. One approach is to use the simple notion of input/output changes. Greater efficiency means reducing input cost—the effort or time required to achieve a given level of output. Greater effectiveness means achieving better-quality or higher-value output for the same level of input. A further guideline for defining useful metrics is to divide them into three distinct categories:

• **IT efficiency** → Direct total cost of ownership (TCO) savings in use of IT resources

• **Business efficiency** → Productivity savings in terms of business users' time to perform both transaction and decision-making work

• **Business effectiveness** → Improved business performance from faster and more informed decision-making

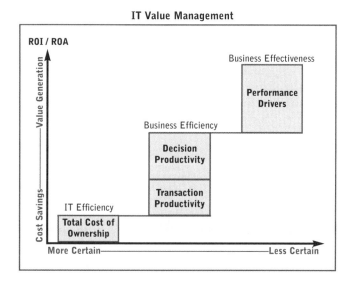

IT Value Management

These three categories include measures ranging from cost savings (efficiency) to value generation (effectiveness), as well as from more to less certainty in the numbers. This is the dilemma and the challenge for IT: the greatest opportunity for ROI and ROA is also the least verifiable, and therefore the least credible.

Hard numbers around IT efficiency, such as cost savings and cost avoidance, are easier to measure and are often the only ones Finance sees as credible. Companies document such costs, or they occur upfront, and therefore involve fewer future projections. Pursuing TCO is a well-established discipline. It captures hidden costs such as implementation, change orders, maintenance, training, and user support. TCO also evaluates common drivers of IT inefficiency such as lack of standardization and consolidation.

Determining the value of business efficiency in user productivity improvements is somewhat harder. However, there are established processes. Historically, IT's primary focus has been on improving efficiency through automation. Cost savings in core transaction processes justified much of the countless dollars spent on technology over the last decade. The heavy investment required to implement enterprise resource planning systems, for example, was usually justified based on the ROI of process improvement that reduced cost per transaction.

However, measuring value merely in terms of IT efficiency from cost savings, or business efficiency from improved transaction productivity, understates the total value. Companies have already achieved most of the major cost savings available from consolidations, platform standardization, and transaction process improvements. While you may still need incremental upgrades and integration initiatives, the bigger opportunity for value is in improving the efficiency and effectiveness of decision-making.

As noted in the introduction, analysis from McKinsey shows that the proportion of more complex decision-based (tacit) work has increased relative to transaction-based work. It now represents more than 50 percent of the workload in many industries.

Unfortunately, decision-based work is much harder to measure, and therefore to determine how to improve. It is information-intensive, interactive, and often iterative. IT must evaluate the value of improving business efficiency and effectiveness around decision-making work. The critical asset— and therefore the element to measure—is information. IT delivers value through quality of information. You measure that quality in terms of relevance, accuracy, timeliness, usability, and consistency. The higher the quality of information, measured across all of these factors, the better the decision-making. This leads to greater user productivity and the ability to drive performance goals.

Some metrics on decision productivity come from monitoring the use of a reporting, scorecard, or overall performance management system. *How many people use it? How often do they use it? When do they use it? How often are reports updated? How many new reports do users create? Who are these power users?* IT can also track user feedback about information quality through self-assessments and qualitative ratings.

Metrics quantifying business effectiveness are in some ways more straightforward, though not necessarily as certain or verifiable. These are based on the performance metrics for the decision area you are improving. As demonstrated throughout this book, decision areas are defined by drivers and outcomes that reflect the cause-and-effect relationships among business issues. This metric hierarchy provides the logic for ROI/ROA calculations and for monitoring success over time.

Barrier 3: *Lack of good decision-making information for managing IT*

IT often lacks its own decision-making information. Beyond the need for metrics noted above, IT needs a context for making a wide range of decisions, as well as for filtering the volume of data it generates. There are two types of IT information sources that are often not fully integrated or harnessed.

The first comes from applications that serve IT processes. Use of information from systems management tools has become quite common, notably to manage security and compliance issues. For example, compliance with Sarbanes-Oxley's Section 404 for General IT and Application Controls involves reviewing access rights, incident logs, change and release management data, and other information generated by IT applications. This information is useful for making decisions beyond compliance.

The second source comes from having more consistent information about the IT management process itself. The Sarbanes-Oxley legislation was a catalyst for well-established best practices in IT becoming more widely adopted. These practices include:

- Frameworks such as Control Objectives for Information and related Technology (COBIT®) from the IT Governance Institute and the Information Technology Infrastructure Library (ITIL) framework

- Methodologies such as the software development life cycle (SDLC)

- Organizations such as the Project Management Institute (PMI).

Greater acceptance and use of these best practices provides more information about IT and the business processes, organizations, and users that IT supports.

The Business of IT

The five decision areas described in this chapter provide IT with insights and facts to help drive overall value for the company.

The sequence of these decision areas provides a logical and iterative flow of analysis and action. The start and end point—IT with a clear view of *where* and *how* it is driving business value—sets the basis for priorities and plans to close gaps. You require a detailed understanding of the effectiveness of IT assets, both individually and combined, to see how to make them more effective. In order to optimize your current assets, or add new ones, you must monitor the projects closely and manage vendors. Finally, you need visibility over the many "moving parts" to ensure you comply with business and regulatory objectives to mitigate risks.

Decision areas on IT:

- **Business value map** → Where and how does IT drive business value?

- **IT portfolio management** → How are IT assets optimized for greatest ROA?

- **Project/SDLC management** → Are projects on time, on budget, on target?

- **IT vendor management** → Are vendor service levels and costs managed optimally?

- **IT compliance management** → Are IT risks and controls managed appropriately?

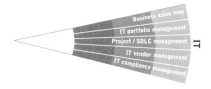

Business Value Map

The business value map provides a high-level view of IT's effect on the business, both currently and potentially. This information sweet spot combines common language with value measurement in a single unifying map for use throughout the company. Of the five decision areas, this is the most important for driving better alignment between IT and the other functions. It helps define the demand for IT and the ways IT can assist. Companies use the business value map at different levels and stages of IT processes. These include defining IT strategy, setting priorities, approving projects and investments, defining requirements, monitoring user acceptance, and validating success.

The business value map provides a consistent understanding of the business and an overall understanding of IT. One useful source of this information is the consistent view of the business required by Section 404 of the Sarbanes-Oxley legislation in terms of organizational entities, transaction processes, systems, people, and their overall relationship to financial accounts.

The business value map provides context and measures gaps in current or projected IT capabilities. This helps clarify the *where / who / how / what / when* questions:

- *Where* are better IT capabilities needed in the company in terms of organizational units, functions, and processes?

- *Who* are the users and stakeholders of better IT capabilities?

- *How* will better IT capabilities drive value for the company (and did they last quarter)?

- *What* are the requirements for developing better IT capabilities?

- *When* must better IT capabilities be available?

This decision area lets you compare strengths and weaknesses in IT capabilities across different business units, processes, and functions. Then you can relate any gaps back to the drivers of performance. *Information quality is a leading indicator of business value—is IT delivering the right information at the right time to the right decision-makers to support the business?* You can evaluate gaps in information quality using a number of qualitative factors. These include relevance, accuracy, timeliness, availability, reliability, breadth of functionality, and consistency. These factors can be used to clarify cost/benefit options and let you prioritize potential improvements.

BUSINESS VALUE MAP

GOALS	METRICS	DIMENSIONS	
Business Priority Score	BI Users (#)	Current/Target Scenario	IT Project Status
Business Value ($)	Business Effectiveness Index	Scenario	IT Projects
Information Quality Index	Business Efficiency Index	Decision Processes	IT Project Type
IT Capability Index	Employees (#)	Business Function	IT Project
IT Costs ($)	Information Accuracy Rating	Decision Area	Key Business
	Information Availability Rating	Employee Decision Role	Information
	Information Consistency Rating	Work Function	Business Subject Area
	Information Functionality Rating	Decision Role	Metadata Model
	Information Relevance Rating	Fiscal Year	Organization
	Information Timeliness Rating	Year	Division
	IT Project Costs ($)	Quarter	Department
	IT Projects (#)	Month	Org. Code
		Information Supply Chain	Strategy Focus
		Information Stage	Strategic Area
		IT Improvement Priority	Strategy
		IT Improvement Priority Rating	Transaction Processes
			Process
			Sub-Process
			Activity

FUNCTION	DECISION ROLES	PRIMARY WORK	CONTRIBUTORY	STATUS
IT / Systems				
	Executives	•		
	Managers	•		
	Analysts	•		
	Professionals	•		
Finance				
	Executives	•		
	Managers	•		
	Analysts	•		
	Professionals	•		
Customer Service				
	Executives			•
	Analysts		•	
Distribution				
	Executives			•
	Analysts		•	
Operations / Production				
	Executives			•
	Analysts		•	
Purchasing				
	Executives			•
	Analysts		•	
Product Development				
	Executives			•
	Analysts		•	
Sales				
	Executives			•
	Analysts		•	
Marketing				
	Executives			•
	Analysts		•	
Human Resources				
	Executives			•
	Analysts		•	

IT Portfolio Management

This is the supply side of the IT value equation, while the business value map decision area is the demand side. Portfolio management offers details of and insights into the company's IT assets, how well these support the business, and what opportunities exist to improve IT ROA spending by:

- Expanding the portfolio by acquiring new IT assets

- Investing more in existing IT assets to generate greater value from them

- Retiring obsolete or inefficient IT assets

- Implementing controls to mitigate risk related to IT assets

While there are many potential categories and attributes of IT assets, the three core ones are infrastructure, applications, and information. Using this decision area, IT can analyze the inventory of physical IT assets (hardware, software, data sources, and applications); their properties (such as vendor and direct cost); and their core capabilities (such as flexibility, scalability, reliability, compatibility, and availability).

GOALS	METRICS	DIMENSIONS	
IT Capability Index	BI Users (#)	Application Software	IT Efficiency Opportunity
IT Costs ($)	Employees (#)	Application Type	IT Savings Magnitude
IT Efficiency Index	IT Asset Availability Rating	Software	IT Savings Type
	IT Asset Compatibility Rating	Data Sources	IT Improvement Priority
	IT Asset Flexibility Rating	Data Source Type	IT Improvement
	IT Asset Reliability Rating	Data Source	Priority Rating
	IT Asset Scalability Rating	Decision Processes	IT Project Status
	IT Direct Costs ($)	Business Function	IT Projects
	IT Indirect Costs ($)	Decision Area	IT Project Type
	IT Project Costs ($)	Discretionary Budget	IT Project
	IT Projects (#)	Fiscal Month	Key Business Information
		Year	Business Subject Area
		Quarter	Metadata Model
		Month	Organization
		Goals/Metrics Hierarchy	Division
		Goal Type	Department
		Goals	Org. Code
		Metrics	Transaction Processes
		Information Supply Chain	Process
		Information Stage	Sub-Process
		Infrastructure Environment	Activity
		IT Technical Layer	
		IT Asset Type	
		IT Asset	

FUNCTION	DECISION ROLES	PRIMARY WORK	CONTRIBUTORY	STATUS
IT / Systems				
	Executives	•		
	Managers	•		
	Analysts	•		
	Professionals	•		
Finance				
	Executives	•		
	Managers	•		
	Analysts	•		
	Professionals	•		
Audit				
	Analysts		•	
Customer Service				
	Analysts		•	
Distribution				
	Analysts		•	
Finance				
	Analysts		•	
Human Resources				
	Analysts		•	
Marketing				
	Analysts		•	
Operations / Production				
	Analysts		•	
Product Development				
	Analysts		•	
Purchasing				
	Analysts		•	
Sales				
	Analysts		•	

Improving IT efficiency, however, is not enough. Most companies have tied 70 percent of their IT budget to non-discretionary items. You can't cut these "keeping the lights on" costs easily. You can gain additional and invaluable insight in this decision area by comparing how diverse IT assets work together to support specific areas of the business. Think of these IT assets as belonging to an information supply chain that acquires, manages, and delivers access to information for end users. Thinking in terms of shared and integrated supply chains delivering information and functionality makes it easier to explain how improvements to incomplete, complex, or obsolete IT assets represent greater effectiveness and value to the company.

IT should set standards and document the core business metadata for the company. Consistent metadata and business rules are critical for information to become a trusted sweet spot in decision-making processes.

Project/SDLC Management

This decision area is one of two that make up IT's operational bread and butter. Value is generated from IT assets by implementing new software and infrastructure or developing new applications. With IT's discretionary budget for new projects limited to about one-third or less of the total IT budget, resources are scarce and expectations high. This makes good information even more critical.

Most IT departments have hundreds of separate projects that are interrelated, overlapping, or at various stages of completion. This decision area tracks the status of major projects against common project management milestones such as scope, requirements analysis, design specifications, development, testing, implementation, and production. Monitoring on-time, on-budget, on-quality project indicators is critical to managing scope, unplanned changes, and necessary adjustments. This information, which may need to be aggregated from several sources, also improves alignment around project priorities and helps flag duplication in purpose or scope.

GOALS	METRICS	DIMENSIONS	
IT Project Completion (%)	External Resource Days (EFT)	Business Scope	Project Start Date
IT Project Lead Time (#)	Internal Resource Days (EFT)	Fiscal Month	Year
IT Project ROI (%)	Initiatives Rejected (#)	Year	Quarter
	IT Project Cost ($)	Quarter	Month
	IT Project Value ($)	Month	Contract End Date
	New Initiatives (#)	Forecast Scenario (Plan/Actual/Forecast)	Project Management
	Proj. Duration (#) – Business Days	Scenario	Project Team
	Proj. Duration (%) – Variance	Investment Range ($)	Project Sponsor
	Rejection Causes (#)	IT Projects	Project Manager
	Total Resource Days (EFT)	IT Project Type	Project Member
		IT Project	Project Completion Date
		IT Project Status	Year
		IT Project Complexity	Quarter
		IT Project Milestones	Month
		IT Project Risk Level	Project Finish Date
			Related Projects
			Organization
			Division
			Department
			Org. Code

FUNCTION	DECISION ROLES	PRIMARY WORK	CONTRIBUTORY	STATUS
IT / Systems				
	Executives	•		
	Managers	•		
	Analysts	•		
	Professionals	•		
Finance				
	Executives			•
	Analysts		•	
Audit				
	Executives			•
	Managers	•		
	Professionals	•		
Customer Service				
	Executives			•
Distribution				
	Executives			•
Operations / Production				
	Executives			•
Purchasing				
	Executives			•
Product Development				
	Executives			•
Sales				
	Executives			•
Marketing				
	Executives			•
Human Resources				
	Executives			•

Contextual dimensions provide greater comparability across different projects. This allows for learning and best-practice sharing between "apples and oranges" by pooling common information about different projects. These dimensions can include:

- Investment amount (< 50K, < 100K, < 500K, > 1M, etc.)

- Complexity (features, information, architecture)

- Dynamic versus static

- Business scope (point solution, departmental, or enterprise)

- Critical skills required

- Risk level (likelihood and impact assessments)

A key benefit of this information is that you gain insights even from failed projects. By seeing what worked and what didn't across many different projects, and by ensuring a full life cycle perspective on development projects, you can avoid future mistakes and resource misallocations.

This information sweet spot helps manage expectations across the team, sponsors, and stakeholders. With it, IT management can avoid project cost overruns, missed deadlines, and subpar quality deliverables. Beyond avoiding the adverse financial implications of failed projects, it also helps IT avoid the potentially serious impact on the company's reputation and credibility.

IT Vendor Management

This decision area represents the other operational information sweet spot for IT. In many companies, IT is second only to Purchasing in terms of dollars spent on external vendors. IT needs a consolidated view of how much it is spending on IT assets and with whom. It's a long list, from PCs and PDAs to routers and telecom services, from software licenses to system integrator services.

Analyzing this information sweet spot helps identify what to consolidate and/or standardize to reduce costs and complexity. It also reveals where you can pool requirements to gain purchasing power or generate higher service levels.

When this information is fragmented across the enterprise, it is difficult to spot duplication of contracts and agreements. Simple comparisons of vendor costs by function and user can help uncover potential excesses. Knowing that other vendors have provided similar products or services also helps IT foster healthy competition and price/quality comparisons.

GOALS	METRICS	DIMENSIONS	
IT Contract Cost ($)	Credit Rating (#)	Application Software	IT Contract Start Date
IT Project Completion (%)	Employees (#)	Application Type	Year
IT Project Lead Time (#)	IT Asset Availability Rating	Software	Quarter
IT Vendor On-Time (%)	IT Asset Compatibility Rating	Data Sources	Month
SLA Performance (%)	IT Asset Flexibility Rating	Data Source Type	Contract Start Date
	IT Asset Reliability Rating	Data Source	IT Vendor Status
	IT Asset Scalability Rating	Fiscal Month	IT Vendor
	IT Direct Costs ($)	Year	IT Vendor Type
	IT Indirect Costs ($)	Quarter	IT Vendor
	IT Project Costs ($)	Month	Organization
	IT Projects (#)	Infrastructure	Division
	IT Vendor Hourly Rate ($)	Environment	Department
	Quality Rating (#)	IT Technical Layer	Org. Code
		IT Asset Type	Transaction Processes
		IT Asset	Process
		IT Contract End Date	Sub-Process
		Year	Activity
		Quarter	
		Month	
		Contract End Date	

FUNCTION	DECISION ROLES	PRIMARY WORK	CONTRIBUTORY	STATUS
IT / Systems				
	Executives	•		
	Managers	•		
	Analysts	•		
	Professionals	•		
Audit				
	Executives			•
	Managers	•		
	Professionals	•		
Customer Service				
	Analysts		•	
Distribution				
	Analysts		•	
Finance				
	Analysts	•		
Operations / Production				
	Analysts		•	
Purchasing				
	Analysts		•	
Product Development				
	Analysts		•	
Sales				
	Analysts		•	
Marketing				
	Analysts		•	
Human Resources				
	Analysts		•	

This decision area is also important in managing service levels tied to major outsourcing contracts, a fixture for many IT functions. All service level agreements have trade-offs between quality, time, and cost. Measuring quality, especially in the more complex Tier 3 contracts that manage and enhance applications, can be a challenge. For example, where Tier 1 agreements may measure service availability, numbers of incidents, and resolution response times, Tier 3 agreements need to address access to and use of information from applications, and how easy and quick it is to make changes. Even knowing when contracts are up for renewal, as well as when you are triggering penalty or incentive clauses, can lead to cost savings or improved service levels.

IT Compliance Management

IT compliance management is a key focus for U.S. public companies. This decision area consolidates information from different compliance initiatives. As noted in Barrier 3, various frameworks and IT best practices such as COBIT and ITIL require general and application-specific IT controls. This decision area requires three common sources of information.

The first is from compliance program management software, such as that used for Sarbanes-Oxley. Similar to the project/SDLC management decision area, this allows IT to ensure that compliance tasks take place and are meeting program milestones.

The second source of information comes from the controls themselves. Of the 34 IT processes across four domains used in COBIT, a subset is required for Sarbanes-Oxley, notably around security and access controls, change and release management, and incident and problem management. In most cases, these controls involve reviewing large volumes of data and flagging exceptions to established procedures.

GOALS	METRICS	DIMENSIONS	
Compliance Completion (%)	Control Effectiveness Rating	Application Software	Infrastructure Environment
Compliance Costs ($)	Controls (#)	Application Type	IT Technical Layer
Material Deficiencies (#)	Exceptions (#)	Software	IT Asset Type
	External Audit Fees ($)	Assertions	IT Asset
Regulatory Compliance (%)	Internal Audit Costs ($)	Control Frequency	IT Control Processes (COBIT)
Risk Level Index	Issues (#)	Control Method	Control Type (App/Gen)
	Items Overdue (#)	Control Objective	IT Domain
	Outsourced Internal Audit Costs ($)	Control Objective	IT Process
		Control Owners	IT Control
	Reg. Audits	Function	Key Control
	Risk Impact Rating	Position	Remediation Status
	Risk Likelihood Rating	Control Owner	Risks
	Sample Size (#)	Control Type	Risk Category
	Significant Deficiencies (#)	Documentation Status	Risk Type
	Tests (#)	Entity	Risk
		Financial Account	Test Status
		Financial Statement Type	Transaction Processes
		Financial Statement Line	Process
		Financial Account	Sub-Process
		Fiscal Month	Activity
		Year	
		Quarter	
		Month	
		In Scope	

FUNCTION	DECISION ROLES	PRIMARY WORK	CONTRIBUTORY	STATUS
Audit				
	Executives			•
	Managers	•		
	Professionals	•		
Finance				
	Executives			•
	Analysts		•	
Customer Service				
	Executives			•
Distribution				
	Executives			•
Operations / Production				
	Executives			•
Purchasing				
	Executives			•
Product Development				
	Executives			•
Sales				
	Executives			•
Marketing				
	Executives			•
Human Resources				
	Executives			•

The third source is metadata itself. Today, companies have mostly manual internal controls. Approximately two-thirds or more are "detective" controls, versus the more reliable "preventive" ones. Detective controls involve reviewing transaction records in both detailed and summary form. For example, reviewing an accounts receivable trial balance is a detective control. In order for greater reliance to be placed on these controls, there must be a clear audit trail linking the source of information with the definitions and business rules that apply. Being able to monitor and analyze which metadata governs which reports and who has access to it creates a more reliable control environment. It also supports the enforcement of existing data architecture standards.

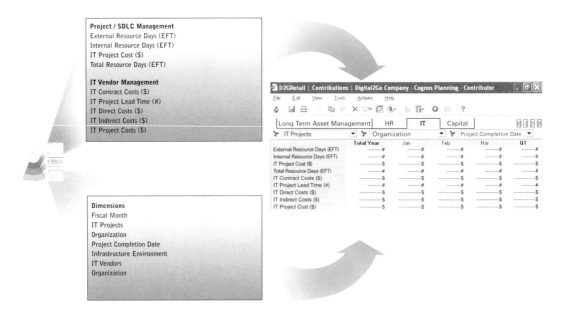

The Project / SDLC Management and IT Vendor Management decision areas illustrate how the IT function can monitor its performance, allocate resources, and set plans for future financial targets.

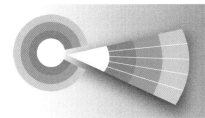

Chief Balancing Officers

*Checking the results of a decision against expectations shows executives what their
strengths are, where they need to improve, and where they lack knowledge or information.*
Peter Drucker

Executive Management bears the ultimate responsibility for the success or failure of the business. Yet
this senior team must work largely by indirect means: setting goals and communicating strategy;
strengthening the organizational culture; recruiting senior talent and building teams; and determining
how to allocate capital, especially for long-term priorities.

The team faces complexity, uncertainty, time pressures, and constraints in its efforts to lead the
organization, and set and deliver on performance expectations. Today, these traditional challenges
occur in the context of unprecedented levels of investor and regulatory scrutiny. Executive
Management must find the proper equilibrium among these pressures, striking the right balance at
the top and causing this influence to pervade the organization.

In the wake of the Sarbanes-Oxley Act (SOX) and other regulatory initiatives worldwide, corporate
governance, risk, and compliance are major focal points for Executive Management. Governance
starts with performance. It reflects the highest-level balancing act for management: *Are we
performing to shareholder expectations?* Risk starts with the flip side of performance: *Are we
successfully taking and managing the right risks to sustain this performance?* Compliance sets the
rules by which we must play: *Are we complying with regulatory requirements?* Executive
Management must understand and balance these business forces to ensure long-term success with
customers, investors, employees, and the law.

Driving your organization's performance is an exercise in balancing:

- Strategic goals and operational objectives
- Financial performance and operational drivers
- Short-term and long-term pressures
- Top-down and bottom-up perspectives.

There are many business approaches that help unlock the right formula: Total Quality Management, Balanced Scorecard, Six Sigma, homegrown variations of these, and more. Such business approaches provide focus, context, and alignment for decisions. They all require the development of a performance management system. This system turns your organizing philosophy into executable actions for decision-makers at the top and throughout the business.

Among the many methodologies and frameworks for defining a performance management system, three basic concepts are universal:

1. How does this action tie back to the financials? (the *so what* question)

2. How does this action tie back to organizational functions and roles? (the *who is accountable* question)

3. How does this fit with the business process? (the *where*, *when*, and *how* question or questions)

While many companies embrace a business philosophy, most lack the performance management system necessary to make it truly successful. Four common barriers prevent Executive Management from striking the right balance in achieving performance, managing risk, and ensuring compliance.

Barrier 1: *Poor vertical visibility of performance drivers*

Executive Management requires a simple vertical hierarchy to connect goals and objectives to underlying functions, processes, and decision areas—including a clear tie back to the financials. This hierarchy is central to a performance management system. With it, Executive Management can understand what has happened, guide today's actions, and plan future performance.

However, despite extensive help in this area (Six Sigma, Balanced Scorecard, Total Quality Management, etc.), companies still struggle with successfully implementing a performance management system. Why? It is difficult to translate the top-to-bottom conceptual logic—goals and objectives, leading and lagging indicators, financial and operational considerations, cause and effect—into practical, measurable areas for which people can feel accountable. The many interrelated factors become too complex to implement or manage.

As this illustration shows, a pyramidal hierarchy ensures a clear, logical path to follow from strategic goals at the enterprise level to operational objectives at the functional level, and then down to specific decision areas within those functions. This reduces the number of goals at the top while building detail at appropriate levels of the organization. This creates a basis for delegating accountability.

The pyramid structure requires a consistency and logic that governs cause-and-effect assumptions. Metadata underpin this consistency, which requires defining appropriate business rules and controlling changes through them.

Barrier 2: *Unclear ownership of performance goals and accountability for them at the front line*

Executive Management is accountable for everything but directly controls nothing. Executives rely on many individuals to strike the right balance and make the right decisions. Micromanaging is maligned for good reasons: it is not feasible for an executive to be everywhere, doing everything; it weakens everyone under the executive, and it distracts the executive from strategy into tactical execution.

Successful leadership thrives in an environment where there is clear ownership of and accountability for results up and down the organization, rather than merely expected tasks and duties. Ownership requires clearly assigned roles in making decisions that drive performance goals and objectives. Accountability requires measuring the value of actions and outcomes. Using the pyramid structure, you can overlay the goal hierarchy with primary and contributory roles in decision-making according to function and decision area.

FUNCTION	DECISION ROLES	PRIMARY WORK	CONTRIBUTORY	STATUS
Finance				
	Executives			•
	Managers		•	
	Analysts		•	
	Professionals		•	
Audit				
	Executives	•		
	Managers	•		
	Professionals	•		
Customer Service				
	Executives			•
Distribution				
	Executives			•
Operations / Production				
	Executives			•

You can assign accountability for these decision areas through the planning process. When you ask people to contribute a target number or set an acceptable threshold for a goal or measure, you have shared ownership of the outcome and helped link the person back to the financial results.

Barrier 3: *Poor horizontal visibility of cross-functional alignment and coordination*

A true performance management system spans more than one function or department. It sits above the business process flow in a related but non-linear fashion. Many performance decisions draw upon different elements across process flows in an iterative way.

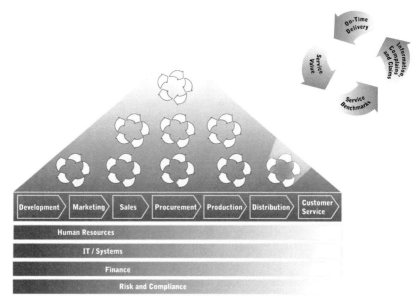

Decision areas overlay the familiar view of core processes and underlying support processes. Each functional set of decision areas provides an iterative feedback loop. Cross-functional sets combine to address additional performance goals and objectives.

If your performance management system adequately captures vertical cause-and-effect relationships, it may still lack visibility across different functions that share common goals or objectives. This visibility is necessary for striking the right balance throughout the organization. Cross-functional or "horizontal" visibility lets decision-makers across business processes collaborate and execute strategy. It also lets Executive Management weigh in on the difficult choices that cannot be resolved at lower functional levels. Delays in cross-functional handoffs and misalignments among departments negatively affect your overall performance.

The performance management system must include two capabilities. First, it must show how everything fits together in terms of business process. Second, it must include a consistent definition of and context for performance drivers across functions that share common goals or objectives. In metadata terms, horizontal consistency means defining common dimensions shared across functional decision-making processes. (For example, it is critical to define and track products, customers, and locations—the anchors of the business—consistently across processes.)

Horizontal Coordination: Conformed Dimensionality Across the Value Chain

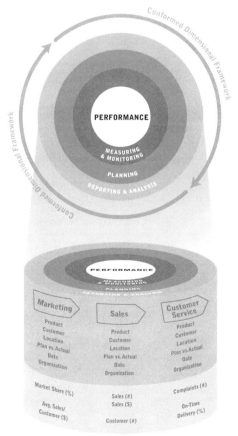

Barrier 4: *Current executive information capabilities do not support the non-linear and iterative nature of decision-making/management processes*

For most employees, decision-making work has increased relative to transaction work, but this situation is not reflected in the information we receive to do our jobs. This problem is most acute in the management process itself. Decision-making should flow top-down and bottom-up in an iterative closed loop. Various decisions in different functions need to be grouped and understood together when they affect the same goals. There are also different decision-making cycles and requirements for long-term strategic goals than for short-term monthly and quarterly operations.

These metrics constantly evolve because 1) they often need tweaking (typically realized by using them), and 2) people's behavior eventually adapts to what is being measured. There is a natural tendency for people to learn over time how to "work the system", which obscures its original intent. This requires agile, adaptive, and controlled metadata functionality of business rules, definitions, and audit trails.

A multi-year strategic management planning process starts by reassessing assumptions and conventional wisdom based on rigorous **analysis**. You must validate or readjust what is important, and should therefore be **measured** and translated into operational **plans** that can be delegated down through the organization. Decision flow then switches to monthly or quarterly monitoring of performance with fast, drill-down analysis and reporting on the underlying causes of results. When these causes have been understood by each of the contributing decision-makers, you can **reforecast** adjustments to operational and financial plans. The bottom line: *You need performance management information at each of these steps to support your decision-makers effectively.*

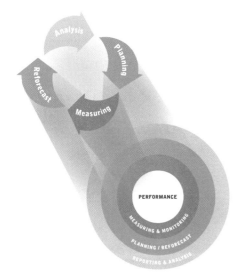

Strategic management cycle:

- **Analysis** ➔ Where do we want to be? (vision and goals)

- **Measures** ➔ What's important? (priorities)

- **Planning** ➔ How do we get there? (objectives and targets)

Operational management cycle:

- **Monitoring** ➔ How are we doing?

- **Analysis and reporting** ➔ Why?

- **Planning** ➔ What should we be doing?

Decision Areas

The six decision areas listed below support the core governance, risk, and compliance balancing act of Executive Management. They include four performance management decision areas and one decision area each for risk and compliance management.

- Performance ➜
    - **Financial management** ➜ Are we performing to shareholder expectations?
    - **Operational revenue management** ➜ Are we driving revenue growth effectively?
    - **Operational expense management** ➜ Are we managing operational expenses effectively?
    - **Long-term assets management** ➜ Are we managing long-term assets effectively to increase future revenue and expense management capabilities?

- **Risk management** ➜ Are we managing the risks of sustaining this performance?

- **Compliance management** ➜ Are we complying with regulatory requirements?

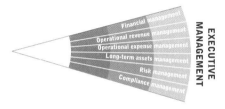

The four decision areas for performance management are further designed to support several interrelated balancing acts: between leading and lagging indicators; between revenue and expense trade-offs; between short-term and long-term resource allocations; and between top-down and bottom-up management processes. Specifically, each of these decision areas has two integrated levels: an overview "dashboard" level and a more detailed operational level.

The latter is an intermediate level that points to other underlying decision areas that contain even more detail, as in the pyramid structure outlined on page 115. It allows Executive Management to gain a comprehensive view of business performance and to zero in on additional detail for greater insight when necessary, then reset targets and plans accordingly. In each case, the set of goals in the overview level dashboard is purposely limited to one illustrative goal per theme, with additional goals and metrics made available at the next drill-down level. Each company will have its own variations on these goals and may determine that more than one indicator should be added at the dashboard level.

Inspired by the Balanced Scorecard framework, the four performance management decision areas provide clear, parallel paths to drill down from goals into their underlying operational drivers. The customer-focused perspective is adapted to include information and metrics from decision areas that drive revenue. The internal process perspective is adapted to focus on operational expense drivers.

The learning and growth perspective also reflects investment and leverage from long-term assets such as human capital and IT assets. The financial management perspective is where we analyze and monitor directly quantifiable financial indicators, but the three other performance management decision areas provide parallel non-financial paths to drill down to operational drivers.

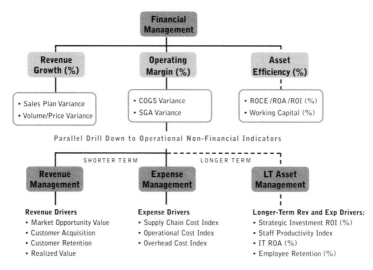

The functions and decision areas described in the rest of this book form a bottom-up framework for designing effective and interconnected information sweet spots of scorecards and dashboards, analytical and business reports, and budgets and plans. Each decision area in this chapter shows a path or starting point for linking the other decision areas together in a top-down logic and, by doing so, establishing cross-functional teams to drive shared goals and objectives. This chapter also highlights the balancing act and trade-offs that Executive Management must make.

Our executive dashboard allows executives to quickly understand the behavior of all the company's revenue drivers. By adding reporting and scorecarding capabilities, we make it easier for decision-makers to manage what matters the most.

Louis Barton, Executive VP, Cullen/Frost Bankers

Financial Management

The financial scorecard is a well-developed information sweet spot for most companies. Its bottom-line results are tied to executive financial rewards and additional incentives such as share options, as well as overall risk factors, to align shareholder expectations with executive team motivation.

The three basic performance measures illustrated here are critical to any business. Revenue growth and operating margin are linked to the statement of income, and asset efficiency is linked to the balance sheet. The fourth is a high-level risk measure. Revenue growth is a key component of shareholder value creation. If costs stay flat, revenue increases will directly affect earnings growth, leading to a positive change in the price to earnings ratio (P/E). Executives and investors watch the operating margin and the associated percentage of operating margin to sales ratio. More sophisticated performance measures include return on capital employed (ROCE), return on assets (ROA), and economic profit. Risk exposure is the flip side of this coin, tracking various categories of risks and mitigating factors that could affect the company's ability to meet its performance goals. These measures more closely align with the investor's perspective, since they give an indication of the risks/rewards generated by a given capital or asset base. Since the capital tied up in the business has a certain opportunity cost for investors, unless these rewards are sufficiently high shareholders will take their cash elsewhere.

Revenue Growth (%)
Is revenue growing? How fast? How does this compare with projections? Executive Management reviews the income statement and the sales plan variance to find out how the business performs against plan, and drills down to find the drivers of any revenue variances. Volume, price, or product mix reasons for sales variances tell Executive Management what other decision areas should be examined. For example, if premium product sales are declining, then Executive Management should review product life cycle management.

Operating Margin (%)
Operating margin is a vital internal performance benchmark. When compared to that of a competitor, it provides a performance comparison for investors. If operating margins are weakening, Executive Management will examine the income statement to determine why. Other margin indicators such as material margin or gross margin help identify which costs are increasing within cost of goods sold (COGS). Operational plan variance may suggest that selling, general, and administrative (SG&A) costs are significantly higher than plan, and the drill-down variance can help determine the cause.

Asset Efficiency (%)—ROCE, ROA, ROI, Economic Profit
Assessing the company's performance through ROCE or similar measures gives Executive Management the same benchmarks that shareholders use to evaluate the business. If the asset efficiency index is not aligned with market expectations, Executive Management can look at causes in the balance sheet or income statement. The CapEx and strategic investments decision areas may highlight when a major plant or equipment investment program has increased the fixed asset base.

Alternatively, by looking more closely at cash flow and working capital, Executive Management may find that accounts receivable delays are negatively affecting working capital. The treasury decision area can give Executive Management confidence that interest on liquid assets such as cash is contributing to asset efficiency performance.

Risk Exposure Index

Executive Management needs a clear understanding of what the company's major categories of risk are and, most importantly, what level of exposure to these risks it faces. Its ability to communicate these risks while instilling confidence in investors and regulators that it is managing them appropriately is critical. In extreme cases, inadequate risk management can cause a company to fail, but risk appetite is what generates returns. Investors expect solid management of it. Risk exposure is a derived metric that shows residual risk after inherent risk has been mitigated.

Executive Management can review changes in exposure and evaluate the potential impact on capital allocation across the business. Drilling down into the risk management decision area gives Executive Management additional insight into inherent risk (such as loss events, loss amounts, or risk assessments), and into the methods of responding to risk (such as avoidance, reduction, sharing, and acceptance).

Likewise, review of compliance management shows the effectiveness of internal controls and the status of current compliance programs and audit activity. Managing compliance is clearly driven by the company's reputation and litigation risks, hence the need for Executive Management to be informed and involved. SOX management is first reported to the Board's audit committee, whose directors, together with company officers, are now more personally liable for financial misstatements and inaccuracies. Directors' and officers' liability insurance rose tremendously after SOX was enacted, precisely for this reason.

We have a number of metrics (data cubes) that help us track profit and loss margins, student and staff details, activity-based costing and asset management. The flexibility of our system has allowed users to drill down from a "big picture" overview provided by our dashboard. This allows us to make decisions on everything from opening up a new offshore campus to minute details like the individual cost of teaching a class of ten students in a particular subject.

Chris Grange, VP Administration, University of Wollongong

Financial Management

Revenue Growth (%)	Operating Margin (%)	Asset Efficiency (%) ROCE / ROA	Risk Exposure Index

Revenue Growth (%)

Income Statement
Goals
• Actual vs. Plan Variance ($/%)
• Net Sales ($)
• Operating Profit/EBIT ($/%)

Drill-Down Variance
Goals
• Profit Change ($/%)
• Sales Change ($/%)
• Volume/Price/Mix Variance ($/%)

Sales Plan Variance
Goals
• Sales Order ($)
• Sales Plan ($/%)

Operating Margin (%)

Income Statement
Goals
• Actual vs. Plan Variance ($/%)
• Net Sales ($)
• Operating Profit/EBIT ($/%)

Drill-Down Variance
Goals
• Profit Change ($/%)
• Sales Change ($/%)
• Volume/Price/Mix Variance ($/%)

Operational Plan Variance
Goals
• Operating Cost Variance ($/%)
• Overhead Cost Variance ($/%)
• Prod. Cost/Sales Ratio (%)

Asset Efficiency (%) ROCE / ROA

Income Statement
Goals
• Actual vs. Plan Variance ($/%)
• Net Sales ($)
• Operating Profit/EBIT ($/%)

Balance Sheet
Goals
• Capital Employed ($)
• Debt to Equity Ratio (%)
• ROCE (%)

CapEx and Strategic Investments
Goals
• Investment ($)
• NPV ($)
• ROI (%)

Cash Flow and Working Capital
Goals
• A/R Days (#)
• Net Cash Flow ($/%)
• Working Capital Ratio (%)

Treasury
Goals
• Borrowing Cost (%)
• Investment Yield (%)
• Net Liquidity ($)

Risk Exposure Index

Risk Management
Goals
• Loss Incidents (#)
• Loss Value ($)
• Risk Level Index
• Risk Mgt. Audit Score

Compliance Management
Goals
• Compliance Completion (%)
• Compliance Costs ($)
• Material Deficiencies (#)
• Materiality Rating
• Regulatory Compliance (%)
• Risk Level Index

SALES   FINANCE   EXEC. MANAGEMENT

Operational Revenue Management

Revenue performance is a key driver of shareholder value. Executive Management must focus on managing revenue goals and directing the business and its resources to the most profitable revenue opportunities. This requires cross-functional cooperation.

Growth requires looking beyond current revenue performance to new opportunities. The strategic plan for growth involves Marketing, Sales, and Product Development. Executive Management looks at the business's ability to acquire new customers in order to generate new sales, and compares this to existing customer retention performance.

Market Opportunity Value ($)

While you may structure your business along functional lines, revenue opportunities cut across Marketing, Sales, and Product Development. By clustering the decision areas associated with market opportunities, you allow more complete and aligned decision-making. This important business driver allows you to develop an overarching index or series of indicators to describe performance. If needed, Executive Management can drill down further into specific decision areas and the related goals and metrics.

If market opportunity value tracks below an acceptable level, Executive Management may look for new market opportunities. For example, a new premium segment growing at 20 percent annually is clearly attractive but the business may have no relevant product offering. The competitor position assessment indicates a low level of competitor consolidation, suggesting it would be easy to gain share. Product and Portfolio Innovation has evaluated the costs necessary to enter this premium segment. Available market and customer feedback gives some confidence that these new product concepts could hit the mark. Executive Management can now assimilate this information and decide the best way forward.

Customer Acquisition (%)

Revenue management is also concerned with the effectiveness of customer acquisition strategies. This means becoming well versed in sales results and the expectations for future sales pipeline and demand-generation activities. If you have weak customer relationships, increasing customer visits by Sales may be a solution. The customer acquisition percentage lets Executive Management monitor this key performance area.

Executive Management must closely scrutinize product life cycle management to see if new products deliver the projected sales results. Most companies launch new products with high optimism. Executive Management must be particularly attentive to early performance indicators. If projected sales are not delivered, you must find out why and communicate this to all levels of the organization. Sales plan variance becomes an essential information sweet spot for determining the *why* and *where* of problems, allowing for a decision regarding the *what*. You must explain these findings well enough that the Board has confidence in the proposed measures, and also be detailed enough to allow lower levels of the organization to execute effectively.

Customer Retention (%)

Growing business revenue is not enough if sales leak away due to poor customer retention. If the customer retention index is low, Executive Management must focus on the operational and service performance issues that directly affect customers. Early indicators of potential problems are likely to come from inadequate on-time delivery performance and from complaints and claims. Monitoring these early indicators informs the team and helps ensure accountability from those responsible. Service benchmarks also offer insights into customer service problems that need to be managed. These benchmarks may also indicate the relative service performance differences between the business and its competitors, highlighting disadvantages that could lead to customers switching despite consistently good service performance.

Despite positive numbers in these early-warning measures, the sales results decision area may indicate poor results, with decreasing sales to existing customers. The solution may be rebalancing sales tactics. Perhaps you need a greater emphasis on improving the specification information to improve customer confidence when making an order.

Realized Value ($)

Realized value provides an overview of the effect on profit of the effort going into driving revenue growth. The customer/product profitability decision area is an important sweet spot for Executive Management. You must review unprofitable customers and pursue different strategies if they are important to the business. A pricing review may indicate that increasing product prices for a large but unprofitable customer would be a bad decision, since this would accelerate the competition's penetration of that market. Reviewing the service cost of the service value metric could highlight too much spending on service support. In that case, you might attempt to negotiate a higher service charge to maintain existing service levels.

Executive Management may also examine product profitability to determine realized value performance. You may look at options to correct the underperformance of loss-making products. These could include discontinuing a product, increasing the price, or changing sales tactics. Increasing prices for certain niche products may offer a "milking" option in the short term to counteract losses somewhere else. Compensating for losses by increasing profits elsewhere is a common decision area in the Executive Management balancing act.

With our performance management solution, we have a simple and quick environment which can handle all our needs and gives us insight into operating costs per cost center and product, sales in relation to the budget, internal purchasing support, premiums paid and disbursed insurance sums. We've increased our reliability and reduced the time spent on certain operations from 66 hours to three. In the long term, this means we'll save masses of time and money thanks to this solution. We are now able to focus 85 percent of our attention on strategic initiatives that help drive our business.

George Janson, Business Intelligence Coordinator, Controller Division, Folksam

---

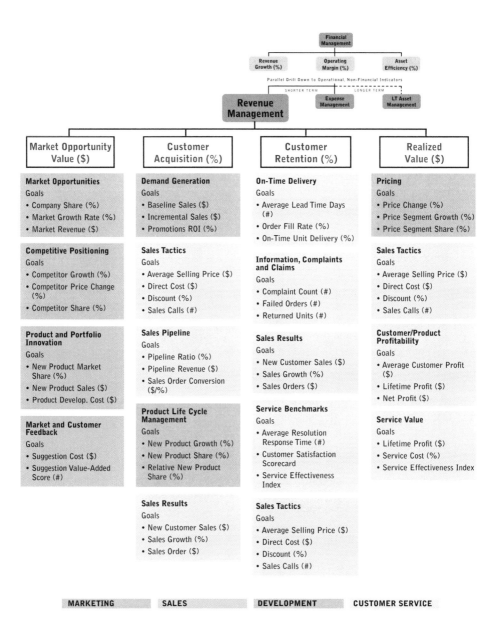

Financial Management

| Revenue Growth (%) | Operating Margin (%) | Asset Efficiency (%) |

Parallel Drill Down to Operational, Non-Financial Indicators

SHORTER TERM — LONGER TERM

Revenue Management

Expense Management — LT Asset Management

Market Opportunity Value ($)

Market Opportunities
Goals
• Company Share (%)
• Market Growth Rate (%)
• Market Revenue ($)

Competitive Positioning
Goals
• Competitor Growth (%)
• Competitor Price Change (%)
• Competitor Share (%)

Product and Portfolio Innovation
Goals
• New Product Market Share (%)
• New Product Sales ($)
• Product Develop. Cost ($)

Market and Customer Feedback
Goals
• Suggestion Cost ($)
• Suggestion Value-Added Score (#)

Customer Acquisition (%)

Demand Generation
Goals
• Baseline Sales ($)
• Incremental Sales ($)
• Promotions ROI (%)

Sales Tactics
Goals
• Average Selling Price ($)
• Direct Cost ($)
• Discount (%)
• Sales Calls (#)

Sales Pipeline
Goals
• Pipeline Ratio (%)
• Pipeline Revenue ($)
• Sales Order Conversion ($/%)

Product Life Cycle Management
Goals
• New Product Growth (%)
• New Product Share (%)
• Relative New Product Share (%)

Sales Results
Goals
• New Customer Sales ($)
• Sales Growth (%)
• Sales Order ($)

Customer Retention (%)

On-Time Delivery
Goals
• Average Lead Time Days (#)
• Order Fill Rate (%)
• On-Time Unit Delivery (%)

Information, Complaints and Claims
Goals
• Complaint Count (#)
• Failed Orders (#)
• Returned Units (#)

Sales Results
Goals
• New Customer Sales ($)
• Sales Growth (%)
• Sales Orders ($)

Service Benchmarks
Goals
• Average Resolution Response Time (#)
• Customer Satisfaction Scorecard
• Service Effectiveness Index

Sales Tactics
Goals
• Average Selling Price ($)
• Direct Cost ($)
• Discount (%)
• Sales Calls (#)

Realized Value ($)

Pricing
Goals
• Price Change (%)
• Price Segment Growth (%)
• Price Segment Share (%)

Sales Tactics
Goals
• Average Selling Price ($)
• Direct Cost ($)
• Discount (%)
• Sales Calls (#)

Customer/Product Profitability
Goals
• Average Customer Profit ($)
• Lifetime Profit ($)
• Net Profit ($)

Service Value
Goals
• Lifetime Profit ($)
• Service Cost (%)
• Service Effectiveness Index

MARKETING   SALES   DEVELOPMENT   CUSTOMER SERVICE

Operational Expense Management

Once customers have made orders, there is little scope for operating errors without affecting profit margins. With approximately 90 percent of revenue going into making and delivering a product or service, information that helps Executive Management identify operating anomalies and act quickly can make the difference between success and failure.

By grouping relevant functional decision areas together, the information sweet spots can be aligned with typical business concerns. These business challenges need to be approached cross-functionally and cannot be solved in isolated silos.

Business is a process that starts with inputs and ends with outputs. In between, you must manage value-added activities for efficiencies and costs. On the input side, this starts with supply chain efficiency, followed by the internal operating processes needed to produce a product or service. You manage these internal operating processes by monitoring operating costs, reflecting the key driver in achieving sustainable profits. Organizations carry a number of support functions broadly classified as overhead. You must manage these overhead costs to ensure that, for example, departmental headcounts do not grow out of control, and that your various support activities deliver real value. When you have a finished product, you must distribute and deliver output, bringing the cycle back to supply chain efficiency.

Supply Chain Cost Index

This index highlights the balancing act between input and output for management. The unpredictable is the norm. No sooner have purchase orders gone out for next month's requirements than you see changes in expectations. The sales plan variance metric reflects future sales expectations; if it indicates an unexpected increase in orders, Procurement and Purchasing must respond. If suppliers are not sufficiently responsive to the unexpected increase in orders, meeting the order surge may become a problem that Executive Management must address by looking at, for example, ways to announce possible delivery delays and the impact of these on customers.

As a manufacturing company we are faced with constraints. We have a seasonal business and limited production capabilities as well as limited warehouse space. So we have developed a model where we put our sales forecast against our production forecast to monitor machine utilization, target inventory levels, and warehouse space utilization. In that model, because we are rolling out a forecast for several months, we can determine that we are going to face issues in July and address them in March instead. We have been able to move from an annual plan with a quarterly reforecast to a continuous planning process. This lets us get our information to the users quickly so that they can react to that information.

Roberta Kaplan, Director of Business Intelligence, Constar International, Inc.

Financial Management

| Revenue Growth (%) | Operating Margin (%) | Asset Efficiency (%) |

Parallel Drill Down to Operational, Non-Financial Indicators

SHORTER TERM — LONGER TERM

Revenue Management · **Expense Management** · LT Asset Management

Supply Chain Cost Index

Purchasing / Procurement
Goals
- Purchase Price/Unit ($)
- Reject Rate (%)
- Supplier Timeliness (%)

Distribution and Logistics
Goals
- Damaged Units (%)
- Distribution Cost ($)
- On-Time Unit Delivery (%)
- Price/lb/100 miles ($)

Inventory Management
Goals
- Inventory ($)
- Inventory (days/%)
- Inventory Turns (#)
- Product SKUs (#)

On-Time Delivery
Goals
- Average Lead Time Days (#)
- Order Fill Rate (%)
- On-Time Unit Delivery (%)

Information, Complaints and Claims
Goals
- Complaint Count (#)
- Failed Orders (#)
- Returned Units (#)

Sales Plan Variance
Goals
- Sales Order ($)
- Sales Plan ($/%)

Operations Cost Index

Production and Capacity
Goals
- Backlog (%)
- Capacity Utilization (%)
- Systems Up-Time (%)

Cost and Quality Management
Goals
- Failure Cost ($)
- QC Reject Rate (%)

Product Development Milestones
Goals
- Product Develop. Cost ($)
- Product Develop. Lead Time (#)
- Project Completion by Milestone (#/%)

Operational Plan Variance
Goals
- Operating Cost Variance ($/%)
- Overhead Cost Variance ($/%)
- Prod. Cost/Sales Ratio (%)

Information, Complaints and Claims
Goals
- Complaint Count (#)
- Failed Orders (#)
- Returned Units (#)

Project / SDLC Management
Goals
- IT Project Completion (%)
- IT Project Lead Time (#)
- IT Project ROI (%)

IT Vendor Management
Goals
- IT Contract Cost ($)
- IT Project Completion (%)
- IT Project Lead Time (#)
- IT Vendor On-Time (%)
- SLA Performance (%)

Overhead Cost Index

Income Statement
Goals
- Actual vs. Plan Variance ($/%)
- Net Sales ($)
- Operating Profit/EBIT ($/%)

Organization and Staffing
Goals
- Avg. Tenure Years (#)
- Employee Turnover (%)
- Headcount (#)

Cost and Quality Management
Goals
- Failure Cost ($)
- QC Reject Rate (%)

Operational Plan Variance
Goals
- Operating Cost Variance ($/%)
- Overhead Cost Variance ($/%)
- Prod. Cost/Sales Ratio (%)

Benefits
Goals
- Benefit Cost Increase (%)
- Benefit Costs ($)
- Benefit Costs/Payroll (%)

| OPERATIONS | CUSTOMER SERVICE | IT | PRODUCT DEVELOPMENT |
| HUMAN RESOURCES | SALES | FINANCE | |

The ability to see across the supply chain indicators helps Executive Management understand the overall situation. Poor on-time delivery can highlight a problem that may also be reflected in inventory management. The surge in orders may create an inventory problem that Executive Management must decide either is temporary or requires an increase in warehousing capacity. Information, complaints, and claims may indicate risk and exposure with certain customers. Temporary problems in warehousing can be solved by looking at distribution and logistics management. Increasing the carrier capacity and using the distribution network to offset the lack of internal warehousing capacity may be a solution that avoids extra warehouse costs.

This ability to see the whole supply chain and derive information from different decision areas is essential to good leadership. When Executive Management understands the various tolerances and risks, it can confidently make an informed decision.

Information gaps are not acceptable reasons for failure.

Operational Cost Index

Executive Management uses operational cost to monitor the operation's backbone and the related cost implications of inefficiencies and bottlenecks. For example, if you approve a new transaction system, how can you manage and monitor its implementation effectively? In the project management software/system development life cycle (SDLC) decision area, a clear plan will outline the scope of work and time needed to implement the new system. Executive Management must watch cost and time overruns, and perceived risks. You can use the service vendor management decision area and its indicators of past vendor performance to mitigate risks and make better forecasts.

If the purchase order process is difficult—causing system rejections, delivery delays, and an increase in complaints and claims—Executive Management can look at production and capacity management. With the information from this sweet spot, it can assess the implications of using overtime to push delayed orders through. You can gauge cost implications from the operational efficiency and quality management decision areas. The increase in operating costs will affect the operational plan variance. Executive Management will use this information to communicate the discrepancy from plan and focus on solving this problem.

The above example illustrates the importance of managing the unforeseen by using fact-based indicators. Every business has to be ready for the unexpected. Companies that manage these situations as they occur gain a significant advantage.

Overhead Cost Index

Monitoring support functions with the overhead cost index ensures the balance between cost and value makes sense. If this area underperforms, you can analyze the organization and staffing decision areas to look at headcounts, or the income statement to review more detailed functional costs. Management analyzes ratios to understand the cost changes and the relative importance of various support functions or departments. For example, percentage of marketing costs to sales and percentage of sales headcount to total headcount will tell you whether marketing or selling resources are changing in proportion to the business. Increasing sales revenue unaccompanied by an increase in Marketing or Sales headcounts could affect future customer relationships and sales prospects.

The sales plan variance gives Executive Management a key indicator to determine future resource requirements and support costs. If you expect strong sales growth, then this insight can be used to look at the operational plan variance. Senior management can take a more active role in deciding if future sales growth requires broad resource upgrades in the support functions. You can integrate the associated increase or decrease in costs into the planning process. Fast, proactive decision-making increases competitive capabilities across the organization.

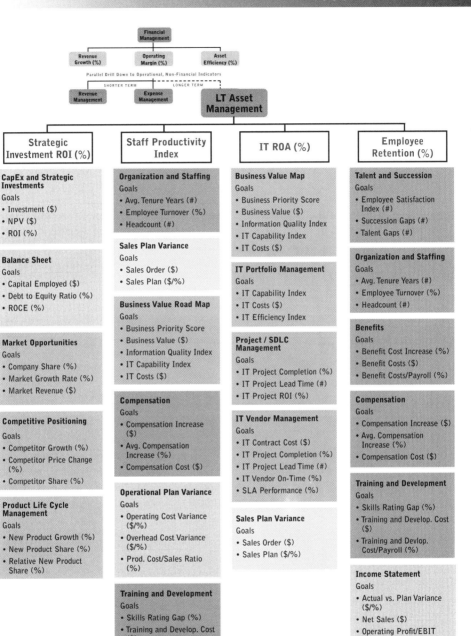

Financial Management

Revenue Growth (%) | Operating Margin (%) | Asset Efficiency (%)

Parallel Drill Down to Operational, Non-Financial Indicators

SHORTER TERM — LONGER TERM

Revenue Management | Expense Management | **LT Asset Management**

Strategic Investment ROI (%)

CapEx and Strategic Investments
Goals
- Investment ($)
- NPV ($)
- ROI (%)

Balance Sheet
Goals
- Capital Employed ($)
- Debt to Equity Ratio (%)
- ROCE (%)

Market Opportunities
Goals
- Company Share (%)
- Market Growth Rate (%)
- Market Revenue ($)

Competitive Positioning
Goals
- Competitor Growth (%)
- Competitor Price Change (%)
- Competitor Share (%)

Product Life Cycle Management
Goals
- New Product Growth (%)
- New Product Share (%)
- Relative New Product Share (%)

Staff Productivity Index

Organization and Staffing
Goals
- Avg. Tenure Years (#)
- Employee Turnover (%)
- Headcount (#)

Sales Plan Variance
Goals
- Sales Order ($)
- Sales Plan ($/%)

Business Value Road Map
Goals
- Business Priority Score
- Business Value ($)
- Information Quality Index
- IT Capability Index
- IT Costs ($)

Compensation
Goals
- Compensation Increase ($)
- Avg. Compensation Increase (%)
- Compensation Cost ($)

Operational Plan Variance
Goals
- Operating Cost Variance ($/%)
- Overhead Cost Variance ($/%)
- Prod. Cost/Sales Ratio (%)

Training and Development
Goals
- Skills Rating Gap (%)
- Training and Develop. Cost ($)
- Training and Devlop. Cost/Payroll (%)

IT ROA (%)

Business Value Map
Goals
- Business Priority Score
- Business Value ($)
- Information Quality Index
- IT Capability Index
- IT Costs ($)

IT Portfolio Management
Goals
- IT Capability Index
- IT Costs ($)
- IT Efficiency Index

Project / SDLC Management
Goals
- IT Project Completion (%)
- IT Project Lead Time (#)
- IT Project ROI (%)

IT Vendor Management
Goals
- IT Contract Cost ($)
- IT Project Completion (%)
- IT Project Lead Time (#)
- IT Vendor On-Time (%)
- SLA Performance (%)

Sales Plan Variance
Goals
- Sales Order ($)
- Sales Plan ($/%)

Employee Retention (%)

Talent and Succession
Goals
- Employee Satisfaction Index (#)
- Succession Gaps (#)
- Talent Gaps (#)

Organization and Staffing
Goals
- Avg. Tenure Years (#)
- Employee Turnover (%)
- Headcount (#)

Benefits
Goals
- Benefit Cost Increase (%)
- Benefit Costs ($)
- Benefit Costs/Payroll (%)

Compensation
Goals
- Compensation Increase ($)
- Avg. Compensation Increase (%)
- Compensation Cost ($)

Training and Development
Goals
- Skills Rating Gap (%)
- Training and Develop. Cost ($)
- Training and Devlop. Cost/Payroll (%)

Income Statement
Goals
- Actual vs. Plan Variance ($/%)
- Net Sales ($)
- Operating Profit/EBIT ($/%)

MARKETING | IT | HUMAN RESOURCES
SALES | FINANCE

Long-Term Asset Management

Long-term investment and asset decisions represent Executive Management's opportunity to influence the future direction and success of the business. This is where the right investment choice can fundamentally redefine both the revenue opportunities and cost efficiencies of an organization. Unfortunately these important decisions are both costly and risky. Senior management has to decide carefully which investment options have priority. The uncertainties involved in these long-term investment decisions are difficult to balance against a backdrop of short-term performance pressures. Failure is not a palatable option, resulting in a lower share price, restructuring and, at the extreme, corporate failure.

What are long-term assets? From a balance sheet perspective, they are defined in terms of property, plant and equipment, investments, etc.—but from an executive perspective they also must include intangible assets such as human capital and IT capability and infrastructure. Designing key measures that offer a holistic perspective on these investments (tangible and intangible) allows Executive Management to monitor the long-term health of the corporation.

Strategic Investment ROI (%)

The strategic investment ROI percentage tracks strategic projects. This sweet spot lets Executive Management learn from the past and adapt those experiences to future decision-making.

Strategic investment decisions, for example an acquisition, require input from a number of decision areas. The market opportunity decision area may have identified an attractive adjacent market segment. You may build a case for the acquisition if existing options for the business are limited and product life cycle management shows poor performance of new products. The case for acquisition strengthens if your existing product portfolio does not have new high-performers and there is little prospect of generating satisfactory growth. If the competitor assessment decision area has identified a potential acquisition target that satisfies corporate due diligence, you then require financial evaluations. Through the CapEx and strategic investments decision areas, Executive Management can review scenarios with associated ROI assumptions. If these conform to the corporate investment structures, then Executive Management must consider whether the balance sheet is strong enough to finance the acquisition. *Should you increase debt or is it necessary to raise additional capital from new shares?*

The above example reflects the type of information sweet spots that Executive Management requires in order to make strategic investment decisions. By making strategic investments a dedicated sweet spot, it can monitor investment performance and rationale for a decision. Acquisitions fail in financial terms due to overpaying for the target or poor execution when consolidating the business. With Executive Management well informed by past acquisitions of the key factors that influence success or failure, you reduce the risks for the future.

Staff Productivity Index

Human capital is a key asset of any business, and Executive Management must track this asset's productivity. A basic assessment reveals headcount and sales per employee by department, but there can be many added levels of sophistication in this tracking. Understanding the context for changes in staff productivity requires Executive Management to seek information from a number of decision areas.

If this indicator increases, implying improved staff productivity, Executive Management should look at how to sustain it. The sales plan variance decision area may show an increase in sales versus expectations, and organization and staffing information will help Executive Management see if and where additional staff were employed. If overall headcount has not increased and an assessment of the compensation decision area indicates stable staff expenses, you know your staff is more productive. The business value road map may confirm that a recent project implementation has had a direct and positive impact on staff productivity. You may have seen an associated increase in training and development expenditures due to the new project, but the result directly improves the staff productivity index. With these figures, Executive Management can push for a review of plans and have other functions record the impact in operational plan variance.

IT ROA (%)

Sudden technology shifts can upend the business model, so Executive Management must know where and how IT assets are driving value across different business units, lines of business, and functions. Comparing the upward or downward trend in IT ROA with current financial and operational results lets you see potential weaknesses in IT strategy. Likewise, comparisons with staff productivity and strategic investment percentages highlight the level of alignment with long-term business goals. If IT ROA is declining in a high-performing area of the business, a drill-down on the business value road map may indicate what specific drivers of performance are at risk, such as revenue growth or operating margins. Understanding *who* is affected leads to a more productive and proactive approach.

Employee Retention (%)

Retaining employees saves money on recruitment and start-up costs; keeping the right employees builds one of your most important assets. The talent and succession review decision area provides additional information for Executive Management, making it aware that new people and talent are necessary to improve the capability of the business. Designing a blend of internal career advancement and strategic recruiting of new talent is an Executive Management priority.

If the employee retention percentage is a concern, you may examine compensation and benefits information, looking at market comparisons. Overall staff cost-to-income ratios provide high-level benchmarks for senior management to compare against competitors. Do you increase staff costs, with the associated effect on the income statement, to reverse a weak employee retention index? Perhaps low employee morale is the cause. If so, improving compensation may not actually change employee retention. In this case, it may be more productive to invest in employee team-building or other employee development programs. Training and development information may help to set an appropriate strategy.

Risk Management[1]

Recent regulatory trends such as Basel II for financial services and SOX for publicly traded organizations have heightened the importance of better risk management. So have trends like globalization, integrated financial markets, the knowledge economy, and political uncertainty. The resulting competitive environment and constant rapid change have created countless potential threats to business performance. Today, more than ever, how well you take and manage risks affects your cost of capital through:

- Investors and major exchanges such as NYSE and NASDAQ
- Lenders and related rating agencies such as Moody's and S&P
- Insurers and related loss control programs and coverage discounts.

This decision area provides a consolidated view of several categories and hierarchies of risk, such as operational, credit, and market risk. In addition to these, organizations must monitor environmental and natural risks that impact disaster recovery and business continuity. Having a single integrated universe of identified risks that cuts across common organizational units, functions, and business processes enables more coordinated and cost-effective risk responses.

The trend toward an integrated view of risk has gained ground as the costs of compliance have increased, in particular due to SOX. Many enterprise and operational risk frameworks are available, including the so-called COSO II, which identifies four high-level objectives that frame risk management components, as shown in this exhibit from their Enterprise Risk Management – Integrated Framework, published in 2004. The cube visual reinforces the multidimensional nature of risk management and compliance.

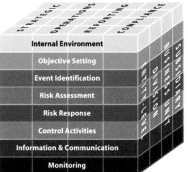

- The four objectives – strategic, operations, reporting, and compliance – are represented by the vertical columns.

- The eight components are represented by horizontal rows.

- The entity and its organizational units are depicted by the third dimension of the matrix.

Ideally, this decision area combines both qualitative and quantitative information. Qualitative risk ratings and assessments are more reliable and verifiable when they are underpinned by numbers that measure risk incidents, events, and loss amounts. Setting accepted risk thresholds, modeling expected outcomes, and monitoring actual results ensures finer insights and tweaking for managing risk.

---

[1] As a subject, risk management warrants a book of its own. Accordingly, this decision area is only meant to provide an overview of what could easily be several more detailed information sweet spots. Also, although it is represented here as a drill down within Executive Management, many companies have a separate risk management function.

For many risks, such as those related to SOX, specific internal controls are in place to mitigate risks. This decision area helps to flag the controls that are most effective and reduce inherent risk to a more acceptable exposure of residual risk.

Risk management is more than tracking obscure or unlikely threats. When risks are tracked against a common map of the business, it is easier to establish the relationship between business performance and risk, like flip sides of the same coin. Insuring common operational risks, notably in Human Resources and Finance, is another area of overlap. For example, the escalating costs of employee benefits and uncertainty in workers' compensation claims are forcing companies to negotiate more self-insurance offerings from their insurance carriers, requiring close analysis and monitoring of reserves-to-losses trends. Likewise, determining the right price for insured cash flow programs requires similar analysis of bad debt reserves.

GOALS	METRICS	DIMENSIONS	
Loss Incidents (#)	Claim Payments ($)	Control Objective	Product Line
Loss Value ($)	Claim Payments (#)	Control Objective	Product Line
Risk Level Index	Claims Aging (#)	Credit Limit Range	Risk Response
Risk Mgt. Audit Score	Control Effectiveness Rating	Range	Response Type
	Country Risk Rating	End Customer Location	Response
	Credit Balance ($)	Region	Risk
	Default Rate (%)	State/Province	Risk Category
		County	Risk Type
	Environmental Risk Rating	Postal Code/Zip Code	Risk
	Est. Loss Incidents (#)	Fiscal Month	Strategy Focus
	Est. Loss Value ($)	Year	Strategic Area
	Intrinsic Risk Rating	Quarter	Strategy
	Occupational Risk Rating	Month	Transaction Processes
	Operational Risk Rating	Information Supply Chain	Process
	Residual Risk Rating	Information Stage	Sub-Process
	Risk Impact Rating		Activity
	Risk Likelihood Rating		Organization
	Write-off Amount ($)		Division
			Department
			Org. Code

FUNCTION	DECISION ROLES	PRIMARY WORK	CONTRIBUTORY	STATUS
Product Development				
	Executives			•
	Analysts		•	
Sales				
	Executives			•
	Analysts		•	
Marketing				
	Executives			•
	Analysts		•	
Human Resources				
	Executives			•
	Analysts		•	
IT / Systems				
	Executives			•
	Analysts		•	
Purchasing				
	Executives			•

Compliance Management[2]

Managing compliance is the key operational execution area of risk management. Even when addressing purely regulatory requirements, the frameworks that guide compliance are often based on a risk perspective. For example, SOX program management uses the COSO framework for defining internal controls requirements based on identifying risks of financial misstatement. Likewise, non-SOX internal audit programs are also anchored in initial risk assessments that suggest which areas of the business require audits.

Ideally, compliance management provides an integrated view of the entire regulatory universe. Most companies face numerous overlapping regulatory requirements. In banking, certain business processes are scrutinized by the Office of the Controller, Basel II, the Patriot Act, and SOX alike. Knowing *where* and *how* to leverage the same controls for multiple regulatory reporting can save you considerable effort in compliance.

As in IT compliance management, this decision area can draw on more than one data source. The first is compliance program management solutions, such as for SOX, that manage a company's projects and programs to ensure compliance. The second source is a new category of tools, often referred to as continuous controls monitoring software, that generate real-time or near real-time information about transactions and flag any exceptions to expected outcomes, as defined by internal controls. For example, inconsistent accounts payable patterns in terms of purchase order numbers or amounts that are just below authorized levels might indicate fraud.

Finally, compliance management can also draw information from solutions that automate manual spreadsheet-based processes, including reports that are used to perform detective or monitoring control activity. The most common and costly, from a compliance perspective, are manual financial reporting and close processes, in particular for consolidation and adjustments.

We've always had good visibility and control of our financial house. As a publicly traded company on the NASDAQ (in the U.S), we are subject to the intense scrutiny required by Sarbanes-Oxley. In this light, good is no longer good enough. We have to be great.

Tom Manley, CFO, Cognos

---

[2] As compliance can span several regulatory areas, this decision area is only meant to provide an overview of what could easily be several more detailed information sweet spots. Also, although it is represented here as a drill down within Executive Management, many companies have a separate internal audit function reporting directly to the Board's audit committee.

COMPLIANCE MANAGEMENT

GOALS	METRICS	DIMENSIONS	
Compliance Completion (%)	Controls (#)	Application Software	Fiscal Month
	Exceptions (#)	Application Type	Year
Compliance Costs ($)		Software	Quarter
	External Audit Fees ($)	Assertions	Month
Material Deficiencies (#)	Internal Audit Costs ($)		
Materiality Rating	Issues (#)	Control Frequency	In Scope
		Control Method	Key Control
Regulatory Compliance (%)	Items Overdue (#)	Control Objective	Regulators
	Outsourced Internal Audit Costs ($)	Control Objective	Regulator Type
Risk Level Index		Control Owners	Regulator
	Qualitative Materiality Rating	Function	Remediation Status
		Position	Risks
	Quantitative Materiality (%)	Control Owner	Risk Category
		Control Type	Risk Type
	Reg. Audits	Documentation Status	Risk
	Risk Impact Rating	Entity	Test Status
	Risk Likelihood Rating	Financial Account	Transaction Processes
	Sample Size (#)	Financial Statement Type	Process
	Significant Deficiencies (#)	Financial Statement Line	Sub-Process
	Tests (#)	Financial Account	Activity

FUNCTION	DECISION ROLES	PRIMARY WORK	CONTRIBUTORY	STATUS
Finance				
	Executives			•
	Managers		•	
	Analysts		•	
	Professionals		•	
Audit				
	Executives	•		
	Managers	•		
	Professionals	•		
Customer Service				
	Executives			•
Distribution				
	Executives			•
Operations / Production				
	Executives			•
Purchasing				
	Executives			•
Product Development				
	Executives			•
Sales				
	Executives			•
Marketing				
	Executives			•
Human Resources				
	Executives			•
IT / Systems				
	Executives			•

SUMMARY

We reviewed thousands of performance management initiatives in writing this book. Organizations successfully engaging with performance management were able to align resources, opportunities, and execution to gain a sustainable competitive advantage.

Alignment requires a unifying map and a common language. That is what the framework in this book is about. This shared framework supports and strengthens the business/IT partnership, and the partnership between decision-makers in different decision areas across different business functions. It offers a single viewpoint on customers and suppliers, products and brands, and the business results. It ensures people in one division are looking at the same information as people in another.

Three fundamental requirements enable this alignment and successful performance management:

Information Sweet Spots
The issue is not getting more data—people are drowning in data—the issue is getting the right information. The key is to design, group, and enrich data into information sweet spots. Information sweet spots help managers make the best revenue growth decisions, the best expense management decisions, the best financial management decisions, and the best decisions for long-term asset management.

Managers Perform Within Collaborative Decision-Making Cycles
Decision-makers need to achieve their objectives in the context of the company's objectives. Information and strategy must be communicated in multiple directions, not just one way. Information sweet spots link executive management and line management. They connect decision-makers throughout the organization and let them understand, manage, and improve the business.

Integrated Decision-Making Functionality in Different User Modes
Each decision is a process rather than an event. Once you see *what* has happened, you may need to analyze it to understand *why* it happened. You must put the occurrence in context to see trends common to other parts of the business, geographies, product lines and, most important, objectives. From there, you can see the way forward and plan the future of the business.

The Performance Manager

Decision-makers need integrated information at their fingertips to focus on winning, rather than the distraction of gathering information. This requires a system to deliver performance management information whenever and wherever they require it.

Knowing what's happened and why it happened, aligning this knowledge with objectives, and articulating a plan to establish a forward view of your business—these are the skills of a performance manager. This book provides a framework to design information sweet spots that will drive your business performance. We hope you will use these concepts to surpass the results achieved by performance management initiatives from around the world.

The right information at the right time can make all managers better; but more importantly, it can make good managers great. Letting people realize this untapped potential is why we wrote this book. We hope your personal and business successes drive our next edition.

Roland P. Mosimann
Chief Executive Officer, BI International

As CEO and co-founder of BI International, Roland has led major client relationships and thought leadership initiatives for the company. Most recently, he drove the launch of the Aline™ platform for on-demand Governance, Risk, and Compliance. Roland is also a co-author of *The Multidimensional Manager* and *The Multidimensional Organization*.

Prior to founding BI International, Roland was a member of the Executive Board of the World Economic Forum in Geneva. Responsible for leading the financial services and supply chain management sectors of the Forum's activities, he worked with Chief Executive Officers and cabinet-level government officials in North America, Europe, and Asia. He was a consultant with McKinsey & Company in Zurich, and he served in Singapore as Market Executive for Tetra Pak's Asian sales operations.

Roland holds an MBA from the Wharton School of the University of Pennsylvania and a B.Sc.(Econ) from the London School of Economics.

About Business Intelligence International

BI International is a global expert in providing the frameworks, structures, and analytics that allow businesses to properly manage risk and performance.

Since 1995, with *The Multidimensional Manager* and subsequent DecisionSpeed® framework, BI International has pioneered core principles for aligning information needs with roles, decision-making processes, and cascaded goals to drive performance. In 2004, BI International also launched its Aline™ Platform for on-demand Governance, Risk, and Compliance. These Software as a Service (SaaS) solutions seek to 'right size' Fortune 1000 capabilities so they become affordable for small and medium sized companies.

For more than 10 years, BI International has led the development of key business intelligence solutions for companies both large and small across the Financial Services, Manufacturing, Pharmaceutical, and other industries. Beyond its direct customers, BI International has influenced thousands of companies worldwide through its thought leadership, frameworks, workshops, and design tools. For more information, visit the BI International Web site at **www.aline4value.com**.

Meg Dussault
Director of Analyst Relations and Corporate Positioning, Cognos

Meg started her marketing career in 1990, beginning with campaign management for the national telecommunications carrier as deregulation was changing the market. She then moved to market development for Internet retail and chip-embedded smart cards before moving to product marketing with Cognos.

Since joining Cognos, Meg has worked extensively with executives and decision-makers in the Global 3500 to define and prioritize performance management solutions. This work was leveraged to help shape the vision of Cognos performance management solutions and to communicate the message to key influencers.

About Cognos

Cognos, the world leader in business intelligence and performance management solutions, provides world-class enterprise planning and BI software and services to help companies plan, understand and manage financial and operational performance.

Cognos brings together technology, analytical applications, best practices, and a broad network of partners to give customers a complete performance system. The Cognos performance system is an open and adaptive solution that leverages an organization's ERP, packaged applications, and database investments. It gives customers the ability to answer the questions—*How are we doing? Why are we on or off track? What should we do about it?*—and enables them to understand and monitor current performance while planning future business strategies.

Cognos serves more than 23,000 customers in more than 135 countries and its top 100 enterprise customers consistently outperform market indexes. Cognos performance management solutions and services are also available from more than 3,000 worldwide partners and resellers. For more information, visit the Cognos Web site at **www.cognos.com**

Patrick Mosimann
Founding & Joint Managing Director, PMSI Consulting

As co-founder of PMSI (Practical Management Solutions & Insights), Patrick has led major client engagements and has significant experience across several industry sectors.

His prior experience includes consulting at Strategic Planning Associates (now Mercer Consulting), working on projects in Banking, Telecoms, and other industries. He also worked at the investment bank Morgan Grenfell (now Deutsche Bank) and with Arthur Andersen on audit assignments in Europe.

Patrick also holds an MBA from the Wharton School of the University of Pennsylvania and a B.Sc. (Econ) from the London School of Economics, University of London.

About PMSI

PMSI provides practical and commercial solutions to drive performance with data-driven decision-making using a combination of business consulting skills, data integration, and analytical capability.

The design of a successful performance management solution requires the expert understanding of the business decisions and drivers across various responsibilities and functions. PMSI acts as a bridge between the insights needed within a business and the potential IT capability and delivery. The focus is to fully leverage the innovative use of technology and create highly repeatable, business-led solutions while reducing cost of delivery.

PMSI's experience ranges across industry sectors and markets; this cumulative business knowledge and flexibility of solution and approach is of particular value to its clients. For more information, visit the PMSI Web site at **www.pmsi-consulting.com**

Acknowledgments

The authors would like to acknowledge the many outstanding companies and individuals who have contributed to the publication of *The Performance Manager* and agreed to share their experience publicly:

BCBS Tennessee	Frank Brooks	Kotányi GmbH	Andreas Speck
Bloorview Kids Rehab	Hakim Lakhani	Ministry of Defence	Henk van Tigchelhoven
C & C Ireland	Paul Rainey	Mölnlycke Health Care, US, LLC	Susan Dean
Coloplast GmbH	Marina Glodzei		
Constar International, Inc.	Roberta Kaplan	Pernod	Vincent Meunier
Cullen/Frost Bankers	Louis Barton	Philips	Eelco van den Akker
Delta Sonic Car Wash	Chris Boebel	Prysmian	Russell Garnett
Diageo (Dubai)	Narayana Rao	Raiffeisen International Bank-Holding AG	Michael-Hagen Weese
ENECO Energie	Ton van den Dungen		
FOD VVVL (Federal Government Department of Public Health, Food Chain Safety and Environment)	Georges Leenen	Reichle & De-Massari	Markus Pfister
		Ricoh	Nur Miah
		Suncorp Metway	Alex Mongard
		University of Wollongong	Chris Grange
Folksam	George Janson	Vesuvius Group	Nicolas Mathei
Générale de Protection	Mikael Perhirin	WEKA Verlag AG	Niolas Schloesser
Jeans West	Patrick Aldred		

From within our own respective organizations, we want to thank the many individuals who have supported the authors, provided thought leadership and 'real world' input for the development of the framework and the writing of the book.

From Cognos, we want to thank Dave Laverty and the management team: Jane Baird, Doug Barton, Drew Clarke, Sue Gold, Chris Kaderli, Dave Marmer, Leah MacMillan, Mychelle Mollot, as well as Forrest Palmer, Rich Lanahan, Rob Rose, Tahnia Sanchez, David Pratt, Tom Manley, Kathryn Hughes, Dr. Greg Richards, Peter Griffiths, Robert Helal, Tom Fazal, Farhana Alarakhiya, Leo Tucker, Jon Pilkington, and Eric Yau.

From BII, Dominic Varillo, Richard Binswanger, Justin Craig, Rich Fox, Bob Hronsky, and Bob Marble.

From PMSI, Steve Whant, Nicolas Meyer, David Crout, Jeremy Holmes, Tim Bowden, and Andrew McKee.

In addition, we want to recognize the years of framework refinement shared with Art Certosimo, Matthew Matsui, Cecil St. Jules, Pete Vogel, and Jennifer Cole.

We also want to recognize Rob Ashe for the thinking and work he has done to create and evangelize performance management as a business imperative.

Finally, we would like thank Dr. Richard Connelly and Robin McNeill. They are responsible for the genesis of the principles in this book and have supported and coached us through its writing.